CHINA'S
ECONOMIC
AND
SOCIAL
PROBLEMS

CHINA'S
ECONOMIC
AND
SOCIAL
PROBLEMS

GREGORY C. CHOW
Princeton University, USA

NEW JERSEY · LONDON · SINGAPORE · BEIJING · SHANGHAI · HONG KONG · TAIPEI · CHENNAI

Published by

World Scientific Publishing Co. Pte. Ltd.

5 Toh Tuck Link, Singapore 596224

USA office: 27 Warren Street, Suite 401-402, Hackensack, NJ 07601

UK office: 57 Shelton Street, Covent Garden, London WC2H 9HE

Library of Congress Cataloging-in-Publication Data
Chow, Gregory C., 1929–
    China's economic and social problems / by Gregory C. Chow (Princeton University, USA).
    pages cm
    Includes bibliographical references and index.
    ISBN 978-9814590402 (hardcover : alk. paper) -- ISBN 978-9814590419 (pbk. : alk. paper)
    1. China--Economic conditions--2000–   2. China--Economic policy--2000–   3. China--Foreign
economic relations. 4. China--Social conditions--2000–   I. Title.
    HC427.95.C4893 2014
    330.951--dc23

                                            2014012247

British Library Cataloguing-in-Publication Data
A catalogue record for this book is available from the British Library.

In-house Editor: Elizabeth Lie

Typeset by Stallion Press
Email: enquiries@stallionpress.com

Printed in Singapore

Preface

For decades since I received my PhD degree in economics from the University of Chicago, I was active as an academic economist and an economic adviser to the government of Taiwan from the mid-1960s to the late 1970s and to the government of China from the 1980s to the 1990s. Both kinds of work required serious research. In recent years, my interest has changed to thinking about broader economic issues and problems and possible solutions to these problems. I have served as a columnist for the *First Financial Daily*, and later for the *Southern Metropolitan Daily*, the Chinese edition of *Financial Times*, the Chinese edition of *South China Morning Post* in Hong Kong and *Commercial Times* in Taiwan.

I have published two books as collections of newspaper articles. They are (1) *Interpreting China's Economy* with both Chinese and English editions published by World Scientific and a second Chinese edition published by Zhongxin, and (2) *China as a Leader of the World Economy*, with editions in both languages published by World Scientific and a second Chinese edition published by Truth & Wisdom Press in Shanghai. This book consists of more recent newspaper articles. I hope that readers will provide me with critical comments. This book has four parts, first on economic problems, the second on economic studies, the third on economic policy and the fourth on social problems. By glancing through the table of contents, the reader can get a bird's eye view of the topics covered.

In writing the chapters, I have benefited from critical comments by many friends, including in particular Professors Hu Shouwei and

Wang Zeke of Zhongshan University, Professor Shen Yan of Peking University, Professor Niu Linlin of Xiamen University and Dr. Wang Yi of the People's Bank of China. I am also indebted to Ms. Elizabeth Lie of World Scientific who made a serious effort in editing and in improving the exposition of this book. The financial support from the Gregory C. Chow Econometric Research Program at Princeton University is gratefully acknowledged.

Gregory C. Chow
Princeton, NJ, USA
November 28, 2013

Contents

PART 1

Economic Problems

CHAPTER 1

Historical Tradition and the Present-Day Chinese Economy

In order to discuss this topic, I first refer to an article by Professor Lin Man-houng of Academia Sinica and National Taiwan University, "Important characteristics of China's traditional economy," (Taiwan: Academia Sinica, *Proceedings of Humanities and Social Science*, February 1992) and then raise some relevant questions for the reader's consideration.

The questions discussed in the above article by Professor Lin include:

1. How traditional agriculture and light industry were developed which have affected these productive activities today.
2. How private ownership of land was developed in the period of Warring States while farmers had used the land belonging to the kings during the previous Zhou dynasty.
3. How the family system was formed and how family members worked together that affect the Chinese economy today.
4. How commerce and trade were developed, including international trade. The development of commerce includes different forms of money, the development of industry alongside the expansion of trade, relation between rural and urban economies, commercial organizations, forms of communications and finance, government industrial enterprises and government commercial policy, which are all relevant today.

5. How the governments throughout history exercised their role in economic activities, including the employment of labor for infrastructure building, such as the Great Wall and the Grand Canal, and the provision of loans to poor farmers in certain periods.
6. How morality and the value system were formed and how they affect the working attitude and habit of present-day Chinese workers.
7. The system of economic incentives and social welfare that existed in Chinese history.

In addition, I would like to raise the following questions for consideration:

1. How the political system of China today is affected by its historical tradition and how the development of democracy is affected by China's history. In the annual report by the Chinese Premier to the National People's Congress, progress toward a democratic government has been an important topic. Is China ready for democracy? If so, based on China's historical tradition, what form of democracy is most suitable?
2. How the legal system today is affected by historical tradition, including the legal system established in the Republic of China and practiced to a large extent in Taiwan today. How the legal system introduced since the beginning of economic reform in 1978 affects the traditional use of *guanxi* in business transactions.
3. Does economic planning practiced before and after the economic reform, which began in 1978, have its historical basis, such as the building of the Great Wall and the Grand Canal?
4. How is today's family system affected by China's history, including childbirth, relation between parents and young children, marriage and the relation between retired parents and their children?
5. In Professor Lin's article, historical periods of prosperity and recession were mainly explained by political factors, with good government administration at the beginning of a new dynasty, but we need to consider economic factors, including the effect of government policies such as taxation policy on national output.

6. What were the state enterprises in Chinese history?
7. What were the banking and financial institutions? How were private enterprises encouraged or discouraged?
8. Were there historical precedents to the present-day emphasis on getting rich and being wealthy?

We can understand the present-day Chinese economy better by considering these questions in terms of China's historical tradition.

CHAPTER 2

Development Trends in China's Trade Surplus

Since the mid-1990s, China has had a large trade surplus. This has helped generate aggregate demand to propel China's rapid economic growth. It has also fueled inflation in China because the foreign exchange generated by the surplus was converted into RMB and led to an increase in money supply that caused inflation. Reducing the surplus has the benefits of (1) slowing down inflation in China, and (2) helping the countries exporting to China increase their aggregate demand and GDP, and thus contributing to the world's economic recovery. Therefore, when China's export surplus is reduced, both China and other countries which export to China will benefit. To reduce China's trade surplus, China should allow the exchange rate of RMB to increase, making it more expensive for other countries to buy Chinese goods and less expensive for China to import from other countries.

In recent years, the RMB was allowed to appreciate gradually from 8.3 RMB per US dollar to 6.3 RMB per US dollar as of April 18, 2012. See Figure 1 for the appreciation of RMB against the US dollar. What can this appreciation of RMB and the recent data on China's trade surplus tell us about the world's economic development? This question came to my attention because the International Monetary Fund (IMF) just released a report asking a similar question.

Despite the appreciation of the RMB as given in Figure 1, the recent IMF report says that it is too early to say yet whether the yuan is still "substantially undervalued" and that as global growth returns, China's export surplus will increase. The IMF is seeking additional funding from China to increase its earning capacity.

The IMF has sharply reduced its long-term forecast for China's current-account surplus, a move that could strengthen Beijing's defense against the US view that China's currency is "substantially undervalued." China's current-account surplus fell from a pre-global crisis peak of 10.1% of GDP in 2007 to 2.8% of GDP in 2011, and the IMF described this as a downturn that was "sharper and more persistent than expected." But the IMF said it is still in the process of assessing whether the yuan is in line with market fundamentals.

To judge whether the RMB exchange rate is close to equilibrium, we can observe its trend as given in Figure 1. Figure 1 shows that since the middle of 2011, the exchange rate has been going upward fairly rapidly, more rapidly than from mid-2008 to mid-2011. The recent trend suggests that the rate will continue to go up and has not yet reached equilibrium. If it is allowed to increase upward, the trade surplus will gradually decline. From this trend, the IMF is justified in predicting a sustained reduction of China's trade surplus.

In addition, the IMF has presented an optimistic outlook of China's economic development to which I concur. In its outlook, the IMF noted the appreciation of the yuan and said that continued appreciation and progress in implementing policies identified in the nation's 12th five-year plan would ensure that the recent decline in the external surplus is sustained. The five-year plan, which extends through 2015, includes a mix of policies which include boosting

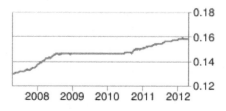

Figure 1.   US$/RMB

household income, domestic consumption and the service sector. Increase in domestic consumption can be achieved by the increase in imports as part of reducing the export surplus. Increasing China's imports would help raise aggregate demand for the exporting countries and promote global economic recovery.

CHAPTER 3

Corporate Social Responsibility

A market economy is known to work because of the invisible hand of Adam Smith: even when different members of the society promote their own economic self-interest, the society benefits because the market coordinates these opposing forces. However, one should not ignore another important aspect of the market economy: the spirit of cooperation and the social responsibility that the members of a market economy take on voluntarily. Part of this is imbedded in the culture of any society. When we grew up in China, for me in the 1930s and 1940s and probably later for most of the readers of this chapter, we all learned to love our neighbors, in addition to members of our own family. Such a sense of responsibility to others also applies to a corporation since a corporation is made up of individuals.

Living in the US, one learns about corporate social responsibility from outstanding examples such as the work of the Ford Foundation. Ford Foundation contributes not only to benefit the American society but also to the welfare of other countries. From 1985 to 1996, it set up a US Committee on Economics Education and Research in China that supported an economics training center at Renmin University during this period and a second training center at Fudan University from 1988 to 1993. The annual budget of this program was about US$1 million. I served as co-chairman of the US Committee while former President Huang Da of Renmin University served as chairman of the corresponding committee representing seven major Chinese universities selected by the State Education Commission (now the Ministry of Education).

11

In the last year or two, I have been fortunate enough to learn about the ideas of corporate social responsibilities from observing the working of the Taiwan Semiconductors Manufacturing Company (TSMC). As most readers know, this company is the world's largest producer of semiconductors. Its main competitors are Intel and Samsung. The company's corporate social responsibilities include its responsibilities towards its customers, shareholders, employees, suppliers and society in general. In its responsibility to the society, it has set up a foundation to help promote cultural activities in Taiwan and has received numerous awards from the Taiwan government for its effort to protect the environment by setting up factories that are environmentally friendly and energy efficient.

On December 14, 2012, TSMC made an announcement to report how the company recognized and appreciated the support and contributions of its suppliers at its 12th Annual Supply Chain Management Forum that was held on the same day. Eight outstanding equipment and materials suppliers were also awarded the Supplier Excellence Award. The theme of the forum was "Innovate and Win Together" and over 450 suppliers around the world in the fields of equipment, materials, packaging, testing, facilities, IT systems and services, export/import services, and environmental and waste management services participated in it.

I have written this chapter for readers in China because as China's economy has been transformed from a planned economy to a market economy, market participants have concentrated on promoting their self-interests. They have contributed to the economic development of China because the invisible hand of Adam Smith has been at work. However, most business enterprises in China have not learned or practiced their social responsibilities and need to be reminded to do so. I hope that this chapter will serve as a small reminder and that the practicing companies themselves and the entire Chinese market economy will benefit from such a practice. In the 1980s, the political leaders in China encouraged some people in China to get rich first with the others to follow. At present, the Chinese leaders seem to encourage the enterprises in China to make money first while believing that the enterprises will develop their social responsibilities in the course of time. However, such a development is slow in coming. In addition, corruption has been rampant among the state-owned enterprises in particular. The problem of corporate social responsibilities in China thus requires our immediate and urgent attention.

Tax Reform in Taiwan and Consumption Tax

Recently, the President of Academia Sinica in Taiwan appointed a committee on tax reform. Its objective is to write a report on tax reform for submission to the government. As the leading research institution in Taiwan, Academia Sinica periodically submits recommendations to the government on matters important for Taiwan's economic and social development. As one of the three advisers to the committee, I would like to present the view of economists on the advantages of a consumption tax and how it can replace the important taxes being levied today for the committee's consideration.

A common tax in many countries is the income tax. However, economists have pointed out that an income tax is undesirable because people are taxed when they produce. To put it another way, work effort, savings and risk taking are all discouraged by an income tax. A more desirable tax is consumption tax, which taxes people when they consume and not when they produce. Sales tax is one such example. Consumption tax would not discourage productive activity. Instead it would encourage savings, making more capital available for investment and promoting economic growth.

In 2012, total tax revenue was 1.6683 trillion Taiwan dollars, with 60.3% from direct taxes and 39.7% from indirect taxes. Direct taxes include individual income tax, corporate income tax and real estate tax. Indirect taxes include consumption tax and tariff. In 2012, individual income tax accounted for 26.4% and corporate income tax accounted for 20.5% of Taiwan's total tax revenue respectively. In 2012, gross domestic product (GDP) equaled 14.0771 trillion Taiwan dollars. Thus, tax revenue equaled 1.6683/14.0771 or 11.85% of GDP.

The tax to be discussed in this chapter is a sales tax proportional to the sales of any commodity. If the commodity is a consumption good, this sales tax is equivalent to a consumption tax. If the commodity is a producer good, the tax will be paid by the producer purchasing that good.

How can Taiwan make a transition to a sales tax? First, the income tax would simply be eliminated. Second, the property tax would be replaced by a tax on the imputed rental value of the property; that is, what the home owner would receive if he rented the home to tenants. This makes sense because the imputed rental value is a measure of the consumption of housing services. Third, the corporate income tax would be eliminated. Under the principle that only consumption and not production should be taxed, a corporation or any productive enterprise should not pay tax on its income or profit. The above sales tax requires a productive enterprise to pay a sales tax on all the inputs it uses. Such a tax would encourage cost saving and increase productive efficiency.

In the following discussion, I will assume that for an output value of 100 dollars, cost accounts for 65 dollars and profit accounts for 35 dollars. When the output is sold to consumers, the consumers pay a sales tax on 100 dollars, and the producer pays a sales tax on 65 dollars. The value added or net output contributed to the economy by the producer is only 35 dollars.

What should the consumption tax rate be? Let us start with an aggregate production function for the Taiwan economy using labor and capital as two factors of production. Assume the contributions of these two factors to GDP are 50% and 50% respectively. For the US, they are 70% and 30% respectively because the US has relative abundance of capital as compared with labor. For China, they are 40% and 60% respectively because China has relative abundance of labor. Let us calculate the tax on personal consumption and the tax on the cost of production as a percentage of GDP. The base of the former is 0.45

if we assume individual income to be 0.5 of GDP and 0.90 of income is consumed. The tax base of the tax on the cost of production is 0.50 (65/35) since the ratio of cost to output is 65/35 and output is 0.5 of GDP. Total tax revenue is therefore based on [0.45 + 0.50(65/35)] = 1.379 times GDP. If tax revenue is set equal to 11.85% of GDP, the required consumption tax rate should be (11.85/1.379)% = 8.593% of GDP. Consumption tax can be collected as a sales tax levied on the consumption of individuals and on the cost of production of business enterprises.

Concerning real estate tax, if the consumer rents his house for consumption and the manufacturer rents his factory for production, real estate tax is already included in the consumption tax as specified above. If the consumer owns his house or the producer owns his factory, a simple way to collect the consumption tax is to collect it as a sales tax when the house or the factory is purchased or built. Strictly speaking, the rental value should be taxed but the purchase value is the present value of all its future rentals generated by the house or the factory. Taxing its purchase value and taxing the present value of all the future rents amount to the same tax.

So far I have not mentioned capital gains. Capital gains are just another form of income generated by investments. Hence, taxing capital gains discourages investments. Under a sales tax, they would not be taxed.

Generally speaking, consumption tax encourages individuals to increase savings, making more capital available for investment and increasing the rate of growth of national output. It encourages cost savings for corporations and improves their productive efficiency. It is easy to collect, avoiding the complications of income tax in filling out complicated tax forms and keeping all receipts for expenditures that are tax deductible.

A possible drawback of sales tax is that it is regressive because low-income people are taxed at the same rate as high-income people while they have to consume a higher fraction of their income. An appropriate adjustment to the welfare system would have to be made. One possibility is for the government to provide low-income people with subsidies to enable them to maintain an adequate level of consumption.

On December 20, 2013, Academia Sinica announced that the rate of growth of Taiwan's GDP in the first three months of 2013 was only 1.93% and that the forecast of the rate of growth for the entire year of 2013 was reduced to 1.80%. If Taiwan's individual income tax and corporate profit tax were replaced by consumption tax and sales tax, the rate of economic growth could be increased.

It is understood that there are many important problems in Taiwan's tax reform which this short chapter cannot cover. I hope that the above discussion on sales tax will be useful in the deliberations of important issues concerning tax reform and economic growth in Taiwan.

CHAPTER 5

Will the Policy to Increase Aggregate Demand by Increasing Consumption Succeed?

The economic growth of China has slowed down recently, with the rate of increase in GDP reducing from over 10% per year in 2008 to about 7.8% per year in 2012. According to the government's one-year plan, the growth rate for 2013 is between 7.5 and 8%. The reason for the decrease is the reduction of exports from China to the rest of the world which has been in a serious recession. Demand for aggregate output of any economy consists of three main components: consumption expenditures, government expenditures and exports net of imports. Reduction of the last component can lead to a reduction in GDP as it has been for China in the last few years. To compensate for the decrease in this component, the Chinese government decided to stimulate consumption expenditures, in addition to its increase in government expenditures by building infrastructures like high-speed railroads.

In this chapter, I try to answer the question whether the government policy to increase aggregate consumption has succeeded or is likely to succeed. My answer is essentially the negative. I will first present some data on the reduction in the ratio of consumption to GDP in recent years. Secondly, I will provide the main reasons for this reduction. If the reasons for the small ratio of consumption to GDP are due to basic characteristics of the behavior of Chinese consumers, it is unlikely that any government policy can change these basic behavioral characteristics. Therefore, the policy to increase aggregate consumption is unlikely to be effective. The above statement is subject to one qualification. Consumption expenditures are composed of private consumption by consumers and government consumption by the Chinese government. The analysis discussed in this chapter applies mainly to private consumption and not to government consumption, although the private component is much larger than the government component.

Statistics on the Ratio of Consumption to National Income

An important reason for the decline in consumption expenditures as a fraction of national income is the increase in uncertainty among the Chinese consumers concerning their future income. Hence, they needed to increase savings to be used for a rainy day in the future when the provisions of social welfare benefits became uncertain. This uncertainty required the consumers to save more for a rainy day in the future. As seen from official data published in the *China Statistical Yearbook* (Beijing: National Bureau of Statistics, 2012), the rate of savings has increased from 37.6% in 2000 to 51.8% in 2011, or the rate of consumption as a fraction of GDP has decreased from 62.3% in 2000 to 49.1% in 2011. As long as the need to save remains the same, the government policy to increase aggregate consumption will not succeed because it is not easy for any government policy to change the basic behavioral characteristics of Chinese consumers. Our analysis also implies that the Chinese government can increase consumption expenditures by improving the social security system but this will take time. Another possible reason is the need to accumulate sufficient funds for sons to get married when there is a shortage of women. If this is the case, such saving behavior will not be affected by any government policy to increase consumption.

One exception to the small amount of consumption expenditures is the sizable amount the Chinese consumers spent in the purchase of new houses in recent years. However, the purchase of new houses and other consumer durable goods should be classified as savings because most part of the purchase is not consumed in one year. When a person purchases a house or an apartment in a given year he does not consume it during that year. The amount of consumption of services from a house in one year consists mainly of depreciation which is only a very small fraction, say 6%, of the value of the house. Hence, the purchase of residential housing by Chinese consumers should be treated as savings for the most part and not as consumption. In recent years, Chinese consumers have saved a lot in order to guarantee their future income.

Perhaps the Chinese government has realized that its policy to stimulate consumption expenditures is not effective and is in the process of changing its policy for the purpose of increasing aggregate demand. One example is the policy to promote the urbanization of China. Since urban residents have higher income than rural residents, such a policy will lead to an increase in the income of Chinese consumers. Increase in income will induce the Chinese consumers to increase consumption expenditures. The new policy is to increase consumption expenditures by increasing consumer income, and not by trying to increase consumption expenditures given consumer income.

CHAPTER 6

Improvement of Health Care in China

We first observe the slow increase in the supply of health care in China by considering several measures of supply given in the table below based on Tables 22–26 and 22–27 of the 2007 *China Statistical Yearbook*. The following table gives numbers of (1) total employed persons, (2) medical/technical persons in health care service, (3) doctors and (4) beds per 10,000 persons in China's health institutions. By comparison, we can easily find the rapid increase in other consumption goods and services during the same period as per capita income increased.

	Total employed persons	Medical/Technical persons in health care service	Doctors	Beds/10,000 persons in China's health institutions
1991	502.5	398.5	15.6	265.5
1996	541.9	431.2	16.2	283.4
2000	559.1	449.1	16.8	290.8
2004	535.7	439.3	15.0	304.6
2005	542.7	446.0	15.2	313.5
2006	562.0	462.4	15.4	327.1

We can see that total number of persons employed was even slightly higher in 1996 than in 2004 and that the number of hospital beds increased by only slightly over 10% during this period. Note the higher rates of increase of these measures since 2004 that help to explain the slower increase in the price of health care during this period.

As real income of the Chinese population increased, their demand for all consumer goods and services including health care increased. If the supply of health care does not increase sufficiently, the price of health care would go up. According to the *China Statistical Yearbook* (Beijing: National Bureau of Statistics, 2012), from 1996 to 2006, the price index of health care services increased by 12.4%, 22.9%, 17.2%, 11.7%, 11.1%, 10.5%, 8.2%, 8.9%, 5.2%, 5.2% and 3.0% respectively. Such a rapid increase in price was remarkable in view of the stability of the consumer price index during these years.

The reason for the supply of health care services to increase so slowly is that in China, health care provision is the responsibility of the national government and the national government gives this responsibility to local governments. Local governments have limited revenue and most of them prefer to use its limited revenue for economic development while providing just sufficient health care to satisfy its responsibility.

A simple solution to the problem of limited supply of health care is to allow and encourage supply by people-operated (*minban*) health institutions. China has for a long time allowed and encouraged (*minban*) schools to supply education even though provision of education is also the responsibility of the government. *Minban* health care institutions will not only increase supply but also provide competition to public health institutions to improve the quality of health care services. I cannot think of any other government policy which is so simple to apply and has so large an effect to improve the economic well-being of the Chinese people. For example, the strategy of Western Development requires a large amount of capital and the performance of difficult tasks in administering development projects. The change of policy on health care is a simple announcement on the part of the central government. In fact in September 2012, China's Minister of Health Chen Zhu announced at an international economic forum in Tianjin that the Chinese government supports such a policy but this policy has been applied only to a small segment of health care institutions.

There are a number of objections to allowing and encouraging people-operated health care institutions. First, it is said that the government would lose control of the provision of health care. This is not the case since the government will continue to regulate the behavior of *minban* health care institutions just as it regulates private industrial and commercial enterprises and *minban* schools. Second, some claim that the provision of health care should be treated differently from the provision of other goods or services because the doctors know more than the patients about what they should want (known as "asymmetric information" between the supplier and the consumer in economics) and therefore can exploit the patients by charging them more than required. This is true to some extent but patients cannot be assumed to be entirely ignorant as they can consult with friends and other doctors. More importantly for what is being discussed in the present chapter, such exploitation by doctors exists as much in public hospitals as in private hospitals.

Third, some consider this policy infeasible because of the resistance of central and local health care officials who may have vested interest in protecting public health care institutions and argue against the establishment of private hospitals. To solve this political problem, the central government does not need to decide in principle whether *minban* health care institutions are desirable or better than public institutions. It only needs to give a green light for them to come forth. If the *minban* institutions are worse than the public institutions, patients will not go to them. The main reason for the success of China's economic reform was to allow nongovernment institutions to compete with government institutions, such as township and village enterprises and private enterprises to compete with state-owned enterprises.

A related objection is that some local governments may be reluctant to encourage *minban* health institutions to operate in their localities. In my proposal, the central government need not interfere with local governments' policy regarding health care except that the right to establish *minban* health care institutions is guaranteed as a national policy. Some local governments may be reluctant to encourage *minban* health institutions or to allow their own hospitals to be leased for private operations. They should have discretion in carrying out their policy regarding how much to encourage the private operation of health institutions. Incentives to rid them of their financial burden and improve the well-being of their people would cause many local governments to adopt this policy, while others will wait and see. The central government can leave the introduction of private health institutions to the discretion of local governments and be confident that if the experiments are successful, more local governments will adopt it.

Before closing, let me stress that this chapter deals only with the supply side of health care. It discusses who provide it, and not how to pay for it. China has recently introduced different ways to improve health insurance policies, which are not the subject of this chapter. One may ask whether health insurance money can be used to pay costs of private hospitals and whether local government subsidies should also be provided to private hospitals. My answer to the first question is "yes" in order to provide competition. To the second question, my answer is the same as what is written in the previous paragraph. It is up to the local governments to decide for their localities. Incentives to increase competition and to improve the well-being of their people would cause many local governments to provide equal subsidies to all health care institutions. It is even better if the subsidies were going to the patients in the form of insurance coverage so that they can decide which hospital to go to. Hospitals charging high prices and offering poor quality will have to improve or they cannot survive.

CHAPTER 7

Increase in Wage in China

In this chapter, I would like to discuss China's wages in recent years, the rate of increase, the reasons for the increase and whether the increase will lead to a reduction in foreign investment, and thus affecting the rate of growth of the Chinese economy.

According to the 2011 *China Statistical Yearbook*, from 2006 to 2010, China's average wage of employees in urban units has increased every year. These wages were 20,856 yuan, 24,721 yuan, 28,898 yuan, 32,244 yuan and 36,539 yuan respectively. Wage increase is due to the increase in national demand for labor.

Wage is the price of labor. Therefore, wage is determined by the demand for and the supply of labor. This chapter discusses only the demand for labor because the supply of labor is determined by the size of China's working-age population which has increased very slowly. The demand for labor is determined by the manufacturer. There are two factors of production, namely, capital and labor. If capital is fixed and only labor is increased then the amount of output resulting from an additional unit of labor will be reduced as the quantity of labor increases. This is known as the law of diminishing returns from labor in economics. The amount of output resulting from an additional unit of labor is known as the marginal product of labor. Factories hire workers in order to increase production. To maximize profit, a factory will hire more workers up to the point where the value of the marginal product of the last worker hired is no less than the wage paid to him. Therefore, the demand curve for labor as a function of wage has a negative slope. That is, if the amount of capital

27

is fixed, in order for the factories to hire more workers, wage must be reduced. If we want to keep wage constant while increasing the demand for labor, the quantity of capital must be increased.

In summary, the demand for labor has two determining factors, which are the quantity of capital and wage. The larger the quantity of capital, the greater the demand for labor. When wage is reduced, the demand for labor will increase. Using this basic theory, we can explain why wages in the United States are higher than those in China. The reason is that the US has more capital per worker than China. The larger amount of capital results in a larger demand for labor and thus a higher wage.

The above theory can be used to explain the demand for labor in China's economic development, and why in recent years, China's wages have increased every year. In the course of economic development, the amount of capital in the economy increases as a result of both domestic and foreign investment. Given the increase in capital, the demand for labor in China has increased and thus wage has increased. In the late 1960s, mainly as a result of the research of T. W. Schultz of the University of Chicago and Gary Becker of Columbia University, a third factor of production known as human capital was added to the theory of production. Human capital refers to the quality of labor. A country's human capital is determined by its history, tradition and investment in education. In this theory, the quantity of human capital resulting from investment in education becomes a third factor of production. The increases in both physical capital and human capital can lead to an increase in the demand for labor and thus an increase in the wage rate, in China and elsewhere.

For decades, China's economic development is fueled by the increase in both physical capital and human capital. Both physical and human capital have increased as a result of domestic and foreign investment. Domestic investment has included investment in both physical and human capital in the form of building of factories and infrastructure and of education. Foreign investment in China contributes not only to the increase in physical capital, but also to the introduction of new technologies and modern management system.

Such investments in physical and human capital have led to an increase in demand for labor and hence wage in China.

Foreign investment has taken place because of the low wages in China. In recent years, some foreign-owned factories have moved to other countries because China's wages have increased. Some people have argued that the increase in wages has resulted in the outflow of foreign investment and is therefore harmful to China. This argument is wrong for two reasons First, the total quantity of physical and human capital in China has been and will be increased. This has led to and will lead to an increase in the demand for labor and thus an increase in the wage rate in China. Second, the increase in wage in China itself is a desirable result of economic development to improve the people's standard of living.

The World Bank and the International Monetary Fund have provided data on per capita incomes of different countries — per capita income in each country is measured in US dollars. The conversion of per capita income to US dollars is not performed by using the exchange rate of the country concerned in terms of US dollars, but by the purchasing power of the domestic currency as compared with the US dollars, i.e. by purchasing power parity. In 2011, China's per capita income was $8,400, as compared with $48,387 in the United States. This reflects the fact that China's per capita capital (including physical capital and human capital) is also much less than the United States. Otherwise, the wage rate and per capita income in China would be much higher. Therefore, the stage of China's economic development is still far behind that of the United States. There is much room for China's wage rate to increase. It would take many years for China's wage rate to catch up with the US wage rate.

Three Models of a Market Economy

In this chapter, I would like to examine three models of market economy — the American model, the Taiwan model and the Chinese model.

First, the American model allows the individual economic units including consumers and producers to have much economic freedom in choosing their economic activities of consumption and production. It allows the market forces of demand and supply to determine prices and outputs. Producers are mainly private enterprises. The role of the government in economic activities is limited, although there are variations among the different economies classified under this model. There are very few government enterprises. The government plays almost no role in promoting special firms or industries. As economists believing in a free market economy often assert, "The government should not pick the winners." The model of Hong Kong is an extreme case, with even more economic freedom than the US model. Hong Kong has an income tax that is about 15% for all individuals, rich or poor, whereas the US has a progressive income tax. The purpose of a progressive income tax is to redistribute income from the rich to the poor. The US has a social security system for the government to provide income to the unemployed and the elderly citizens. In a truly free market economy, these problems are solved by the individual, either with the help of savings or private insurance.

There are different schools advocating different roles for the government in the US. The conservatives, politically represented by the Republican Party, advocate more economic freedom and less government intervention. They believe in lower taxes and lower expenditures for the government. They prefer to use private insurance to solve the problems of unemployment and old age as stated in the previous paragraph. The liberals, represented by the Democratic Party, believe in higher taxes and higher expenditures for the government to engage in more economic activities or to solve more economic problems.

Second, in the Taiwan model, the government is engaged in promoting particular industries. It not only picks the winners but also promotes the winners. In 1973, it established the Industrial Technology Research Institute (ITRI) to engage in applied research and technical services in particular areas. ITRI not only helped selected industries through the provision of particular technological knowhow but also helped to establish particular private enterprises.

To illustrate, Dr. K.T. Li, one-time Minister of Economic Affairs, invited an outstanding entrepreneur in the US, Dr. Morris Chang to head ITRI. Later in 1987, the government supported Dr. Chang in founding the Taiwan Semiconductor Manufacturing Company (TSMC). Through his leadership, TSMC has become the largest silicon foundry in the world with a market cap of about US$100 billion in 2013. Its market cap equals about 11% of the value of all stocks traded in the Taiwan Stock Exchange. The role of the government in promoting the establishment of private enterprises has a long history in China. At the end of the Qing Dynasty, in 1907, Minister of Communications S.Y. Liang initiated and helped a group of entrepreneurs to establish the Bank of Communications which remains to be an important commercial bank in both mainland China and Taiwan today.

Third, the Chinese model allows the state to be even more active than the Taiwan model. The government has changed a formerly planned economy to a more market-oriented economy, but our topic is the model of the Chinese economy as it is practiced today. The government plays a more active role than in Taiwan by establishing and operating state-owned enterprises in important industries. Although private enterprises are allowed to exist in many sectors of the economy, the state enterprises have the additional advantage of receiving government support in terms of subsidies and access to credits from state-owned banks. The role of the state in building infrastructures is more important. Furthermore, the government can engage in projects to change the structure of the economy, including its recent attempt to urbanize the economy by moving some 250 million citizens to newly built cities in the next 10 to 15 years. Some of these projects may be economically inefficient.

In conclusion, one should understand the main reason for the existence of different economic models in different countries. It is mainly the historical background that accounts for the different models which exist in the US, Taiwan, China and other countries today. The reader can confirm this point by reviewing the history of each country.

CHAPTER 9

Five Important Components of the Market Institutions in Chinese Agriculture

China's economic reform began with agriculture. Under the commune system, the farmers produced collectively. A part of the products was delivered to a government procurement agency and the remainder was shared by individual farmers. Production incentive was low because when a farmer worked hard the increase in output was shared by a team of farmers. Under the household responsibility system, a plot of land was assigned to each individual household in a commune. Each household kept its product after a fixed amount was surrendered to the commune. Since taxing a producer by a fixed amount does not affect his incentive to produce, the agricultural output in China increased. During the first six years of reform (1978–84), the annual growth rate of the Gross Value of Agricultural Output nearly tripled to 7.1%. The household responsibility system deals with only the production component of the market. To understand a market economy, we need to discuss four other components. In writing this chapter, I have drawn material from the chapter on Chinese agriculture written by Jikun Huang and Scott Rozelle for the *Routledge Handbook of the Chinese Economy* (London: Routledge, forthcoming) of which I am an editor.

Even in the production component there was the issue of land rights. In the early 1980s, local leaders gave farmers land for 15 years and starting in the 1990s for 30 years. However, village leaders and local governments often reallocated village land for urban development, leading to discontent among farmers. Thus, a secure ownership right is important to production.

The second component is marketing and distribution. After the output is produced, it could be sold to procurement agencies of the government. Allowing the products to be sold in local markets is the second component of the market institutions. Although agricultural commodity markets were allowed to emerge during the 1980s, their number and size were small. In 1984, the state procurement network still purchased more than 95% of the marketed grain and more than 99% of the marketed cotton. Later extension of the market includes export of the products abroad through private export companies.

From 1980 to 2000, the total value of China's agricultural trade grew by about 6.0% on an annual basis. Since 2000, it has more than doubled, making China one of the largest importers of agricultural commodities in the world. Until 2003, the level of agricultural exports exceeded that of imports. Over the past decade, food exports have been growing faster than imports, but, in 2010, China was still largely self-sufficient (97%) in food (including processed food).

Lower tariffs and policies allowing rising agricultural trade began to affect domestic terms of trade in the 1980s. The entrance of private firms to compete in the agricultural trade sector, both imports and exports, has helped stimulate the level of exports of farm products.

The nation's accession to the World Trade Organization (WTO) has helped rural residents and improved incomes, mostly from more liberalized trade agreements that help to increase exports and higher domestic prices.

The third important component is the pricing of the products. Instead of having the prices of agricultural products determined by the government, a market institution requires that the prices be determined by the forces of demand and supply. Farmers' freedom to set prices began as early as 1979. As a result, the relative price of grain to fertilizer rose by more than 60% during the first three years after reform. Price changes had a positive impact on output during the first years of transition; about 10% of the output of rice between 1978 and 1984 came from price effects.

The fourth component is the development of financial institutions to support the development of agriculture. Credit institutions would allow farmers to borrow money to finance production and investment. Unfortunately, there has been negligible progress in the evolution of the rural financial market in China and the provision of financial services is limited. However, most of the farmers are able to carry on their production with little outside financing as China's agriculture output and input markets are mostly dominated by cash transactions.

This was possible with 200 million producers who were engaged in labor-intensive cropping and livestock activities (requiring very little capital) selling to 5 to 10 million super small traders who turned over their inventories in a matter of days, racing from farm to market. Where it was needed, liquidity was supplied by off-farm remittances and by zero-interest loans. Insurance was also provided by diversification, multiple cropping, high levels of irrigation and off-farm earnings.

The fifth component is the role of the government. First, there has been little effort by the government to organize the small farms into larger cooperative organizations. While the rate of growth of production and marketing cooperatives has risen in recent years, only about 20% of China's villages had Farmer Professional Associations (FPA) in 2008 and only 10% of farmers belong to any FPA, far below that of almost all other East Asian nations and many Western nations. Second, research and development (R&D) in agriculture has been provided by the government in developing technology for the farmers. Such effort has been controlled by the state agricultural research system mainly to produce high yields and, after 2000, to improve quality. Only a small share of agricultural R&D in China is performed by the private sector partly as a result of "crowding out" effect from the government programs.

Given the above market institutions, there is strong competition among millions of small farmers and traders. This level of competition has produced agricultural commodity markets that are highly integrated and efficient. Unlike the incomplete market reform in industry, market reform of Chinese agriculture is almost complete.

CHAPTER 10

Three Laws on the Direction of China's Economic Development

There are three important problems in China's economic development. The first is income inequality. The second is environmental degradation. The third is illegal behavior. In the course of economic development, their directions are similar as described by the Kuznets curve.

Simon Kuznets was a famous economist teaching at Harvard University. He discovered that in the course of economic development, income inequality becomes more serious in the early stage and eventually will be less serious at a later stage. Represented by a curve, this phenomenon shows an increasing slope followed by a decreasing slope, or by an inverted U-shaped curve that is known as the Kuznets curve. Besides using the term for income inequality, economists have also used the term for environmental degradation, where it is called an environmental Kuznets curve. In this chapter, I will also introduce the use of this term for the phenomenon of illegal behavior. These three types of Kuznets curves will be discussed in this chapter.

First, about the original Kuznets curve for income inequality, according to an article in the *New York Times* dated July 19, 2013, a survey by Peking University shows a wide gap in income between the nation's top earners and those at the bottom, and a vast difference between earners in top-tier coastal cities and those in interior provinces. The survey found that in 2012, the households in the top 5% income bracket earned 23% of China's total household income.

The households in the lowest 5% accounted for just 0.1% of total income.

According to the survey, "Average annual income for a family in 2012 was 13,000 renminbi, or about $2,100. The average amount in Shanghai was just over 29,000 renminbi, or $4,700, while the average in Gansu Province, was 11,400 renminbi, or just under $2,000. Average family income in urban areas was about $2,600, while it was $1,600 in rural areas." Income inequality has indeed become a serious problem in China.

Note, however, that based on data for the United States, income inequality has increased in recent years, contrary to the proposition of the Kuznets Curve. We will continue our discussion under the assumption that the Kuznets Curve for income inequality may still apply to China.

Second, after economic reform, the environment problem in China has worsened.

To perform a statistical study of the environmental Kuznets curve for China, I have found data on pollution as measured by the volume of industrial gas emission in *China Environmental Yearbook* for the years 1997 to 2005 by provinces. For any given year, the log of gas emission per capita and the log of real income per capita have a positive relationship as suggested by the initial part of the environmental Kuznets curve. Although the observed relationship is for observations among different provinces at one point in time and not for observations in different periods of time, it does describe the effect of increasing income on environmental degradation. It also shows that up to 2005, China had not reached the part of the Kuznets curve with the downward slope. As in the case of income inequality, the stage of China's economic development has not reached the mature stage with a downward sloping Kuznets curve.

Third, the illegal behavior of Chinese citizens has also increased after economic reform started.

People would agree that illegal behavior of Chinese citizens is more serious than in the period before economic reform started and that such behavior is increasing as suggested by the upward sloping part of what I term the illegal behavior Kuznets curve. People may not agree on what explains the seemingly more widespread illegal behavior of Chinese citizens. The illegal behavior includes making counterfeit consumer products leading to illnesses and even death. We have observed Chinese consumers going to Hong Kong to buy genuine products. The illegal behavior also includes the infringement of patent right laws. Furthermore, the behavior of some Chinese government officials in mistreating citizens is also illegal. When Chinese citizens go through legal procedures to protect themselves, they can still be persecuted by central or local government officials who violate the law. Such illegal behavior is partly due to the failure of law enforcement and partly to its economic benefits as the Chinese consumers become richer. The abovementioned illegal behavior is increasing and has not reached the stage with a declining slope in the Kuznets curve.

In conclusion, because of the current stage of China's economic development, the three types of Kuznets curves discussed in this chapter are still in the upward sloping part. The encouraging aspect of our discussion is that all three problems will be improved in the future when their Kuznets curves begin to decline. This happens because when the country becomes richer, its government and people will have the ability to overcome these problems. In Chapter 41, I will discuss how to eliminate corruption. I hope that the Chinese government at different levels and the Chinese citizens, as individuals and as social groups, will make serious efforts to reach the downward sloping parts of these three Kuznets curves to enable the Chinese people to enjoy a more satisfying life.

CHAPTER 11

"China's Economic Empire" from the American Perspective

In recent years, the rapid expansion of China's economic power has attracted attention in the American press. The *New York Times* published an article entitled "China's Economic Empire" on June 2, 2013. I will first state five important points as presented in the article and then discuss their validity.

1. China is taking over the world economically by investing abroad, buying up Western companies such as the American pork producer Smithfield Foods and the French resort company Club Med. China's investment kills jobs in Europe and America. (Why? China's ownership still needs to employ local workers.) China controls oil and gas pipelines from Turkmenistan to China, from South Sudan to the Red Sea, from the Indian Ocean to Kunming and from Siberia to Northern China. China also builds infrastructures like the Merowe Dam on the Nile, Ecuador's Coca Codo Sinclair Dam and other dams all over the globe. Annual investment from China grew from less than US$1 billion before 2008 to more than US$10 billion (in fact about US$55 billion) in the last two years. China's direct foreign investment is projected to be between US$1 and US$2 trillion dollars in 2020.

2. China has become the largest exporter in the world, bypassing the US as the largest trading nation in 2012. By buying mainly natural resources and food, China is ensuring that its two economic

engines, urbanization and the export sector, are securely supplied with the needed resources. In a few years China has become the largest exporter in the steel and solar industries.

3. China's laborers are allowed to work in foreign countries like Denmark's Greenland, partly because there are not enough skilled workers in Greenland to build the needed projects like oil extraction and transportation.

4. China has provided the world with more loans than the World Bank in 2009 and 2010. The loans are used to finance Chinese-built infrastructure and start projects in the extractive and other industries, especially in countries like Angola, Ecuador, Venezuela, Turkmenistan, Sudan and Iran which had difficulties in obtaining loans from the Western countries and the World Bank.

5. China practices unfair competition. Government support, through hidden subsidies and cheap financing, gives Chinese state-owned firms a major advantage over competitors. Since 2008, the Western economic downturn has allowed these firms to gain access to Western markets to hunt for technology knowhow and deals that were previously unavailable to them. While Western companies complain about barriers to investment in restricted sectors in China, Chinese companies enjoy red-carpet treatment in Europe, buying up strategic assets and major companies like Volvo and the German equipment manufacturer Putzmeister. In conclusion, as China becomes a global player and a fierce competitor in American and European markets, its political system and state capitalist ideology pose a threat. It is therefore essential that Western governments stick to what has been the core of Western prosperity: the rule of law, political freedom and fair competition.

The most important development in the modern world in the last century is globalization. Globalization has brought much more benefit than harm to the world. From economics we have learned that free exchanges of goods and services are good for both parties. Globalization consists of exchanges and movement of goods, physical capital, financial capital, labor and technology which accompanies the following four components: trade, investment in physical capital, investment in human capital and movement of labor across countries. The American writer critical of China's economic expansion is essentially criticizing the participation of China in the economic globalization process, as most other countries have done so in the last hundred years. Deng Xiaoping's open door policy has welcomed foreign investment and foreign trade. Both activities have benefited China. There is no reason to criticize China for participating in the globalization process.

The *New York Times* author is also critical of China because it practices unfair competition by state capitalism of the Chinese government. The readers can decide whether this criticism is valid. The topic of the quoted article is economic empire. The word "empire" implies two meanings. The first is the expansion of influence to other countries. The second is forcing other countries to accept such expansion. The first part of this definition applies to China but not the second part. The foreign partners who welcome China's involvement in their economic development through the four components of globalization do so voluntarily. These countries must believe that such voluntary exchanges with China are beneficial to them.

PART 2

Economic Studies

CHAPTER 12

How to Use Econometric Models to Forecast

My PhD thesis at the University of Chicago entitled "Demand for Automobiles in the United States: A Study in Consumer Durables" was completed in 1955 and published as a book in 1957 by North-Holland Publishing Company. In 1958, my thesis adviser, Professor Arnold Harberger (who is still a full time professor at the University of California, Los Angeles while I retired in 2001) proposed to publish my dissertation as well as later dissertations on the demand for durable goods under his supervision as a book. Consequently, *The Demand for Durable Goods* was published in 1960 by the University of Chicago Press. Since my dissertation was already published, I decided to write a paper entitled "Statistical demand functions for automobiles and their use for forecasting" to be included in his book. In the paper, I compared the forecasts based on the equations reported in my 1957 book and estimated using annual data from 1921 to 1953 to forecast automobiles sales in the US from 1954 to 1957. The forecasts based on my equation were quite close to the actual automobile sales in those four years. I needed a statistical test to decide whether the differences between the forecast and the actual sales figures are small enough for us to conclude that the forecasting demand equation remained unchanged after 1953 until 1957. I developed a statistical test to answer such questions and published the work in *Econometrica* in 1960, later known as the "Chow test" that you can find in econometric textbooks. My demand equation was used by General Motors to forecast automobile sales in the late 1950s. Its chief economist Andrew Court informed me periodically about the accuracies of the forecasts, which were good.

Forecasting by econometric equations involve the following steps: (1) formulate an econometric equation or a set of econometric equations based on economic theory; (2) use statistical data to estimate the equations and to make sure that the proposed equations fit the data and (3), assuming the equations remain unchanged in the future, use them to make forecasts. In the example of forecasting sales of automobiles, step (1) was accomplished in my 1957 book. I proposed the hypothesis (new at the time) that the demand for the total stock of automobiles in use (the total number of cars with newer cars given a higher weight than used cars) depends on the relative price of cars (a price index of cars divided by the US CPI) and real income. This is basic economic theory that the demand for a consumer good (for non-durables in particular but also for durable goods if we measure demand by the total stock as I suggested) is negatively related to its price and positively to the consumer's income. Step (2) required gathering data on the quantity of cars in use, a price index (which I had to construct myself using newspaper advertisements since there were no public data available), the US CPI and consumers' income (both published). The above explains the demand for the total stock of automobiles. To explain annual purchases, I utilized the fact that annual purchases are changes in the total stock minus depreciation of the stock during the year. In step (3), I assumed the demand equations to be valid and made some assumptions about prices and income for 1968 to make a forecast of automobile sales in 1968 to be slightly over 8 million cars as compared with the annual sales of about 5 million in the mid-1950s. The forecast for 1968 turned out to be correct.

As a second example, I estimated a demand equation for the total stock of mainframe computers in use in a paper "Technological change and the demand for computers" published in the *American Economic Review* in 1967. A major problem was to construct a suitable quantity index for the variety of computers in use from 1954 to 1965 which my study covered. If there were no new computers introduced in the market, we simply take a weighted average of the quantities in use in any year, say 1964, using their prices in the base year, say 1960, as weights. To deal with new computers introduced after 1960, I had to estimate their hypothetical prices in 1960 when these computers did not exist. This can be done if we assume a stable relationship (an assumption confirmed by Table 1 in the paper) between price and the computer's basic characteristics including (1) multiplication time, (2) memory size and (3) access time. I used the data in 1960 to estimate this relationship. I then used this relationship to estimate the hypothetical 1960 price of each type of computers in 1964, based on the three characteristics. The quantity index for any year is the sum of the quantities of all computer models in use in that year each multiplied by its hypothetical 1960 price. The same idea can also be used to construct a price index for computers in 1964, with 1960 as base year. The price index for 1964 is the sum of the hypothetical 1964 prices of the computers in use in 1960 (as derived by their three characteristics using the relation between the prices of computers in 1964 and the three characteristics) each multiplied by the quantity in use in 1960. In other words, the 1964 price index measures how much the computers in use in 1960 would cost if they were priced in the same way as the 1964 computers, as compared with the actual cost of these computers in use in 1960. IBM had a group of economists doing forecasting and economic analyses for the company. This group used my equation to do forecasting and found the results quite accurate in the late 1960s.

The above method is applicable to explain the demand for desktop or laptop computers, iPhones, iPads and the inputs used in their production. In step (1), we formulate an equation to explain the demand for such products in recent years. The quantity demanded depends negatively on price and positively on the rate of change of income. The reason for using the rate of change of income is based on the finding of my 1957 book on the demand for automobiles. Since the demand for the stock of the consumer products in use depends on income, the new purchase of these products and the rate of change in the stock (minus a small rate of depreciation) depend on the rate of change in income of that year. We can use the idea in the previous paragraph to construct a quantity index and a price index for these products. In step (2), necessary data are used to estimate the demand equation. Accurate forecasting depends on the assumption that the equation formulated remains unchanged in the future and on using good estimates of the price index and the income variable in the equation in the future. These assumptions should be seriously challenged and the challenges should be met before accurate forecasts can be made.

CHAPTER 13

Can Economists Forecast Accurately?

Some people question whether economists can make accurate predictions. I can assure them that economists can really make accurate predictions. When economic theory can explain economic phenomena, these theories can be used to make good predictions. When economic theory cannot explain certain phenomena, these theories would not be able to make good predictions.

To illustrate how knowledge of economics cannot be used to predict economic phenomena, I can cite trading in the stock market and trading in the market for foreign currencies as examples. If economic knowledge could be used to predict changes in stock prices and in the values of foreign currencies, many economists would become rich. Indeed, economic theory tells us that these are unpredictable variables.

The efficient market hypothesis in economics states that once there are opportunities in the market to buy low and sell high to make money, traders will immediately use these opportunities for profit. When all traders can efficiently exploit arbitrage opportunities, trading becomes unprofitable. If a trader has inside information that other traders do not have, then he can profit by trading a particular stock or a particular foreign currency for profit.

An enterprise manager may possess some inside information about his company, say the company's unique invention, and accordingly foresee that the company's share price will rise. If he uses this information to buy the company's stock, he will violate the law. Some government officials may know the appreciation of the national currency in the near future, but the law prohibits them from using such knowledge to sell a foreign currency short and to buy it back when the currency of their country appreciates.

Here I will list some examples in microeconomics and macroeconomics to demonstrate that economic theory can be used to predict accurately. In microeconomics, the theory of consumer demand can be used to explain and predict the demand for consumer products.

For example, in automotive demand, economic theory tells us that the relative prices of cars and the real income of consumers are the main variables to determine the demand. Demand for automobiles is measured by the amount of car ownership. The income elasticity of demand for cars tells us what the percentage change in the demand for automobiles will be when consumer income changes by 1%. Price elasticity of demand for automobile is similar. It tells us how many percentage points the demand for automobiles will change when the price of cars changes by one percentage point. We can use historical data for an economy and econometric methods to estimate these elasticities. Given estimates of income and price in the future, we can use these elasticites to predict the demand for automobiles in the future.

If a person is able to estimate accurately the growth rate of China's national income in the next few years and knows the income elasticity of demand for automobiles, he can use such knowledge to forecast the demand for automobiles in China. Given the rate of growth of China's national income in the past and the demand for automobiles in the past, one can estimate the income elasticity of demand for automobiles. Since the growth rate of national income is quite stable, the knowledge of income elasticity can be used to predict the demand for automobiles in the coming years. I used this method in 1958 to accurately predict car sales in the United States in 1968. My forecast was published in 1960 in *The Demand for Durable Goods* (edited by A. C. Harberger) long before the year 1968 for which the forecast was made. In recent years, the demand for automobiles in China has grown rapidly. I suggest that the same method can be applied to forecast the demand for automobiles in China in the future.

An example in macroeconomics is the forecast of inflation in China. I have estimated an econometric model to explain inflation. First, $\log P$ is explained by $\log(M/Y)$ where P denotes the price level, M denotes money supply and Y denotes national income. A linear equation explaining $\log P$ by $\log(M/Y)$ explains the Chinese data from 1952 onward fairly well. The error in explaining $\log P$ by this equation is denoted by u. If u is positive, it shows that the price level P is above normal and that there is a tendency for it to return to normal in the next year. Inflation is the percentage rate of change in P, or the change in $\log P$. In my model, inflation is explained by three variables: (1) inflation of the previous year showing inertia in inflation, (2) the change in $\log(M/Y)$ since $\log P$ is determined by $\log(M/Y)$ and (3) the regression residual u of the previous year, as explained above.

In 2010, I published a paper in the journal *Economic Letters* entitled "The empirics of inflation in China" to explain this equation in detail. Using this equation, I predicted successfully the rate of inflation in China in 2002 and 2010. This equation was first estimated in 1985. In 1984, China's money supply M defined as currency in circulation increased by 50% in one year. Being concerned with the possibility of inflation in 1985, the then Chinese Premier Zhao Ziyang suggested that I use an econometric equation to predict inflation in 1985 and I estimated the above equation as a result. It predicted only a modest rate of inflation of no more than 9% in 1985 mainly because of the inertia of the low inflation rate in 1984. Later, I used data up to 2009 to re-estimate the above equation and found that, in spite of economic reform after 1978, the parameters of this equation had remained unchanged. I separated the sample into two periods, one from 1952 to 1978 and the other from 1979 onward. Applying the Chow test, I found that the parameters of the above equation remained the same in both periods.

In general, when we question whether economists are able to make accurate predictions, in the same way as whether medical doctors are able to cure patients, the answer is the same in both cases. As a good doctor can successfully cure patients with a serious illness, a good economist is also able to make accurate economic forecasts.

CHAPTER 14

Two Assumptions on Expectations in Econometric Models

The Nobel Prize in 2012 was awarded to two Princeton economists, to Christopher Sims for his contribution to econometric modeling and to Tom Sargent for his contributions to the advancement of the hypothesis of rational expectations used in econometric models.

An econometric model is a set of equations describing the relation of economic variables such as total income Y, total consumption expenditures C and total investment expenditures I. One kind of variables is expectations by economic agents. Consumers will consume more if they believe that their future income will increase; they will consume less if they expect their future income to decrease. In 1957, Milton Friedman published the book, *A Theory of the Consumption Function,* for which he was later awarded the Nobel Prize. In this book, Friedman proposed the theory that aggregate consumption C is proportional to expected income or permanent income Yp. In other words, $C = aYp$. But how is Yp determined? There are two competing hypotheses to determine expected income Yp. Friedman used the hypothesis of adaptive expectations. According to this hypothesis, consumers adjust their expected income each year by a fraction b of the difference $(Y(t) - Yp(t-1))$:

$$Yp(t) - Yp(t-1) = b[Y(t) - Yp(t-1)], \text{ or}$$
$$Yp(t) = b\,Y(t) + (1-b)\,Yp(t-1).$$

From the permanent income hypothesis of consumption $C(t) = aYp(t)$ and the above adaptive expectations hypothesis to determine $Yp(t)$, we can derive the following equation to explain consumption

$$C(t) = abY(t) + a(1-b)\ Yp(t-1) = abY(t) + (1-b)\ C(t-1).$$

I now turn to the hypothesis of rational expectations. By this hypothesis, the expectation for any economic variable is determined by the econometric model itself. In other words, if an economist has a set of equations to explain the working of an economy, this set of equations can be used to generate the expectation of any variable in the model. In the case of the permanent income hypothesis of consumption, the model states $C(t) = aYp(t)$, with $a = 0.8$ for example. Assuming this model to be correct, the economist knows $Yp(t-1)$ last year was simply $C(t-1)/.8$. If permanent income changes slowly by some constant, $Yp(t)$ will be the same as $Yp(t-1)$ but we know $Yp(t-1) = C(t-1)/.8$. Permanent income in year t is a constant + $Yp(t-1)$. Consumption in year t is 0.8 times permanent income in year t. Therefore, $C(t) =$ constant $+ C(t-1)$. This is the permanent income hypothesis of consumption with permanent income determined by rational expectations.

In 1985, I published a paper in the *Journal of Political Economy* to explain consumption and investment of China using data from 1952 to 1983 and found the second version of the consumption function to be valid. I re-estimated the same model using data from 1978 to 2008 and found both the consumption and the investment equations to be valid for both periods. Economic reform beginning in 1978 changed many economic institutions in China but my two equations remained valid for both periods. Recently, I used data for Taiwan from 1951 to 2010 to estimate the consumption and investment equations and found the investment equation to be the same as the one valid for the Chinese economy but the consumption function in Taiwan satisfies Friedman's version of the permanent income hypothesis based on adaptive expectations. I explained the difference by pointing out that the econometric model for Taiwan changed because in 1995, the Taiwan government introduced universal health care insurance which affected the consumption function.

To generalize the above example on the failure of rational expectations, the hypothesis of rational expectations fails whenever the expectation variable in the mind of economic agents is not the same as the mathematical expectation generated by the model. This can happen if (A) the model is not correctly specified, which is the case for many economic models as illustrated by the above model for Taiwan during a part of the sample period. In this case, adaptive expectations can be a better approximation of the expectation of economic agents. Even if (B) the model is almost correctly specified, there is no reason to assume that the economic agents will be so "rational" as to use the mathematical expectation generated by a complicated model as his own psychological expectation. Economic agents may use the simple rule of adaptive expectations to form their expectations.

CHAPTER 15

How to Edit the Handbook of the Chinese Economy?

A handbook is a reference book that covers all important aspects of the subject and explains it in a non-technical way to help an educated reader learn the subject. It may have about 500 to 600 printed pages and include 20 to 25 chapters. For example, a handbook of the Chinese economy may cover different aspects such as the economic reform since 1978, economic growth, economic fluctuations, macro-economic policy, foreign trade, foreign investment, etc. The reader may refer to my book, *China's Economic Transformation* (Wiley-Blackwell, 2007) for the topics covered in 22 chapters although a handbook may have a different list of chapter headings.

Recently, I was asked by Routledge Publishing Company to be the editor for the *Routledge Handbook of the Chinese Economy*. The letter of invitation states the following responsibilities for the editor: (1) developing the initial proposal, including a list of potential contributors for a given list of chapters; (2) suggesting potential members for an editorial board to help review the chapters; (3) contacting potential contributors; (4) ensuring the quality and consistency of contributions; and (5) delivering the manuscript on time.

In the initial proposal I, as editor, will need to provide a list of all important topics of the field and search for potential contributors to write about them. The above tasks seem to be very difficult and time consuming.

I thought of changing the tasks of an editor as specified above to make my role as editor easier. I replied to Routledge by writing:

"I would consider accepting the editorship on the following terms.

1. At Routledge's expense, I will run full-page advertisements in the *American Economic Review* and some other major journals in economics to announce that Routledge is planning to publish a handbook on the Chinese economy with Gregory C. Chow as editor. (This is an advertisement for the handbook itself and justifies Routledge paying for the expense for the advertisements.) Any one interested in serving on the Editorial Board or in submitting a chapter on the subject of his/her expertise should send an email to me. Those wishing to serve on the editorial board should state his/her qualifications as an editor in less than 200 words. Those interested in contributing a chapter should specify the topic of the chapter on which he/she wishes to write and include an abstract of less than 300 words. All respondents should provide a list of five publications in major economic journals. (The last statement helps to screen out applicants who are unqualified.)

2. After receiving a sufficient number of respondents proposing to serve on the editorial board or to write chapters, I will select the members of editorial board and the best (perhaps 50) proposed chapters and distribute them to the members of the board for review. Note that I will not start with a list of chapter headings and seek people to write them but let the chapters come naturally. If I find that certain important areas are not covered, I will ask members of the editorial board to suggest potential contributors."

In two days, the chief editor of Routledge Handbooks accepted my proposal. Compared with the way handbooks published by Routledge and by other major publishers are put together, the above method seems to be much more efficient than the traditional method as specified by the letter which the chief editor of Routledge wrote to me.

Although the above proposal seemed reasonable and efficient, an obstacle was that many economists no longer read articles from printed journals with advertisements. Many read articles from journals on the Internet that have no advertisements. As a result, I decided to think through the important topics and the contributors myself, partly based on my book *China's Economic Transformation* (Wiley-Blackwell, 2007).

The result is a handbook with the following table of content.

1. Historical Economic Institutions by Professor Lin Man-houng of the Institute of Modern History of Academia Sinica in Taiwan.
2. Late Qing and the Republic of China by Professor Kenneth Chan of the City University of Hong Kong. Chapters 1 and 2 provide the historical background of the present-day Chinese economy, covering topics that are similar to the topics of the remaining chapters.
3. China's Planned Economy by Professor Dwight Perkins of Harvard University.
4. The Process of Economic Reform from 1978 by Professor Wu Jinglian of the State Council of China.
5. Economic Growth and Development by Professor Justin Lin of Peking University. Chapters 4 and 5 cover the economic development of the current Chinese economy.
6. Population by Professor Peng Xizhe of Fudan University.
7. Labor by Professor Richard Freeman of Harvard University. Chapters 6 and 7 discuss the topic of human capital.
8. Consumption and Investment by Professor Eden Yu of the City University of Hong Kong and Professor Jean-Pierre Laffargue of the University of Paris.
9. Macroeconomic Policies by Professor Yu Yongding of the Chinese Academy of Social Sciences.
10. Income Distribution and Poverty by Professor Carl Riskin of Columbia University. Chapters 8, 9 and 10 are concerned with the Chinese macroeconomy.

Different economic sectors and institutions are discussed in:

11. Agriculture by Professor Scott Rozelle of Stanford University and Professor Jikun Huang of Fudan University.

12. State and Non-State Enterprises by Professor Ligang Song of Australian National University.
13. Foreign Trade by Professor KC Fung of University California at Santa Cruz.
14. Foreign Investment and China's Investments Abroad by Professor Yasheng Huang of Massachusetts Institute of Technology.
15. Banking and Financial Institutions by Deputy Governor Yi Gang of the People's Bank of China.
16. Legal Institutions by Professor Jacques deLisle of the University of Pennsylvania Law School.
17. Political Institutions and Corruption by Professor Lynn White of Princeton University.
18. Energy and Environmental Policy by Professor Zhang ZhongXiang of the East-West Center.

The handbook concludes with:

19. Prospects of Future Growth and Economic Institutions by Professor David D. Li of Tsinghua University.

The authors of this handbook are selected from the United States, China, Australia, France, Hong Kong and Taiwan. I have also invited Professor Dwight Perkins of Harvard University to be an editor. In my role as editor, I expect to learn from these distinguished contributors.

By April 2014, the page proofs of this Handbook were available for the authors to proofread and the book has been scheduled to be published in 2014.

CHAPTER 16

Comparing Price Movements in Mainland China and Taiwan

In 1985, I began to study price changes in mainland China. In 1984, China's money supply (measured using the currency in circulation) increased by 50%. Hence, the then Chinese Premier Zhao Ziyang was very concerned that inflation could occur. In June 1985, when I arrived at Beijing's Renmin University to start the summer economics course, Premier Zhao sent two officials to tell me his concerns and asked me to study the possibility of China experiencing a serious inflation problem in 1985. I used the annual data from 1952 to 1984 to estimate an equation to explain and predict inflation.

This equation was based on a simple economic theory. The general price index is assumed to be determined by the ratio of money supply to real national output. The greater the amount of money supply, the higher the price index. The greater the national output, the lower the price index. Money supply can be represented by three variables. The first is currency in circulation ($M0$), the second is the first plus demand deposits in banks ($M1$), and the third is the second plus time deposits in banks ($M2$). The definitions of $M1$ and $M2$ were first used in Milton Friedman's money workshop at the University of Chicago in about 1953. I was fortunate to be a student in that workshop.

One may question the validity of my equation because during the period of economic planning which covered much of our sample period, prices were said to be determined by the State Price Bureau. Please note that in 1961 the retail price index in China increased by 16.24% as explained by our theory because the national output in that year decreased by 30%. If we observe the relation of $\log P$, P standing for the price index, to $\log(M/Y)$, Y standing for national output using annual data from 1952 to 2008, we find a linear relation. The deviation u of the observed $\log P$ from the predicted $\log P$ by this equation shows how much the price index deviates from its equilibrium level. If u is positive, there is a tendency for the price index to return to equilibrium in the following period. That is, inflation in period t, as measured by the change in $\log P$ in period t, depends negatively on u at period t-1. My equation to explain inflation has three explanatory variables: the rate of inflation in the last period, the change in $\log(M/Y)$ during this period and u of the previous period. The second variable is justified by the relation between $\log P$ and $\log(M/Y)$.

After estimating such an equation to explain inflation in China using the data from 1952 to 1984, I used it to predict inflation in 1985 and found that the inflation rate would likely be under 9%. The result was reported to the Premier and the study of inflation was published as a paper entitled "Money and price determination in China" in the *Journal of Comparative Economics* in 1987. China's money supply in 1985, 1986 and 1988 was increased by about 35% annually, leading to a serious inflation in the fall of 1988 and much discontent among the Chinese people. From 1985 to 1989, when I was adviser to the Commission for Restructuring the Economic System, we concentrated our effort on institutional reform and did not pay attention to the substantial increase in the money supply during this period. In fact, if any important official in charge of the functioning of China's macroeconomy had paid attention to the rapid increase in money supply during this period, serious inflation in 1988–1989 could have been prevented.

A few years ago, I studied the problem of inflation in China again using data up to 2008, I found that the parameters of my equation to explain inflation remained unchanged if the sample period was divided between 1952–1978 and 1979–2008, as shown by the Chow test of parameter stability. Of course, China's economic reform after 1978 changed many economic institutions in China but it did not change the relation between inflation and its explanatory variables in my equation. The result of this research was reported in *Economics Letters* in 2010. The co-author of this paper, "The empirics of inflation in China," is Professor Wang Ping of the Hong Kong University of Science and Technology.

More recently, I used the same equation to explain inflation in Taiwan from 1961 to 2010, as reported in an article entitled "The empirics of inflation in Taiwan" that was published in *Economic Letters* in 2012. I have found the equation to be capable of explaining Taiwan's inflation and the values of its parameters to be similar to those in the equation used to explain China's inflation. However, the equation used to explain Taiwan's inflation underestimates inflation with sizable errors in 1974 and 1989. The reason is that there were oil crises in those years which raised the prices of imports and the general price index for Taiwan.

CHAPTER 17

Demand for Personal Computers in the United States

In recent decades, the world's most important invention has been personal computers. This invention has affected the life of human beings, not only in work but also in consumption. Consumers can make their purchases online. Economic efficiency has improved in both production and consumption. It is therefore important to conduct an economic study of the demand for personal computers.

The most basic theory in economics is the supply and demand of goods and services. Demand for a consumer good is determined by price and income. The effect of income on demand is positive and the effect of price is negative. Such a theory was first applied to the demand for non-durable goods such as food. To apply it to the demand of durable goods, I suggested in my 1955 doctoral thesis that the same theory applies to the consumption of the total stock of a durable good. The thesis, "The demand for automobiles in the United States: A study in consumer durables," was published by the North-Holland Publishing Company in 1957. For the demand for automobiles, the same theory applies to the total number of cars (weighted by age or quality) in use. The reason is that consumption should be measured by the total stock in use.

The above theory applies to a mature product and may not be applicable to the demand for a new product during the initial years of its introduction. To study the demand for a new product such as mainframe computers in the early years of its introduction from 1954 to 1965, I published a study, "Technological change and the demand of computers" in the *American Economic Review* in 1967. To explain the demand for a new product, I assume the following dynamic adjustment process for the stock Υ_t to reach equilibrium:

$$\log(\Upsilon_t) - \log(\Upsilon_{t-1}) = b(\log \Upsilon_t^* - \log \Upsilon_{t-1})$$

where b measures the speed of adjustment of $\log\Upsilon$ towards its equilibrium level $\log\Upsilon^*$ and $\log\Upsilon^*$ is assumed to be a linear function of $\log P$, P being the relative price of the computers, and $\log(\text{income})$, income being measured in real terms.

I recently used this theory to study the demand for personal computers in the United States for the period from 1993 to 2011. According to the US Department of Commerce Bureau of Labor Statistics, in 1984, 1989, 1993, 1997, 1998, 2000, 2001 and 2003 the percentages of households owning small computers were 8.2%, 15.0%, 22.8%, 36.6%, 42.1%, 51.0%, 56.3% and 61.8% respectively. From these data, one can see that in 2003 the demand for small computers continued to increase.

For the data used, the United States Bureau of Labor Statistics published price indices for two types of personal computers, one for non-portable computers and the other for portable computers. We use a weighted average of these two indices divided by the US consumer price index to obtain a relative price index for personal computers. We use personal income of the US households, also divided by the consumer price index, as the real income variable to explain the equilibrium demand. Quantity of new computers produced each year in physical units is equal to the dollar value of shipment of personal computers produced divided by the above index of average price of personal computers. The value of the computers produced in one year is also given by the US Department of Commerce. What is needed is also the total stock of personal computers Υ in use. It was obtained by assuming a value of 2.8 for 1992 and using the following equation, with t denoting time period.

$$\Upsilon_t = y_t + (1-d)\,\Upsilon_{t-1}$$

where y is the quantity of new purchase and d is the rate of depreciation assumed to be 0.1. To get an initial value of Υ in 1992, we are given the value of y to be 0.4557 in 1993 and can reasonably assume that the value of y to be about 0.4 in 1992. In years before 1992, y had grown rapidly. If we let Υ in 1992 to be 7 times 0.4, the result is $\Upsilon = 2.8$ in 1993.

Using the above statistical data, we have estimated the demand equation for small computers with the following results: The rate b at which the demand in log is adjusted to its equilibrium level is about 0.67. The price elasticity of demand in equilibrium is about 0.64. Income elasticity of equilibrium demand is about 2.3. These are reasonable estimates and the demand equation explains the data well.

I have found the microeconomic theory of demand and supply to be applicable for explaining economic phenomena in different times and in different countries. Examples are given in my book *China's Economic Transformation* (Wiley-Blackwell, 2007). Let me also add that using macroeconomic theory, economists were not able to predict the financial crises and the resulting great recession of the US and Europe after 2008.

CHAPTER **18**

Further on the Demand for Personal Computers in the United States

In Chapter 17, I discussed the demand for personal computers in the United States. That chapter did not report completely my research on this topic. This chapter will report on the remaining part of the research. It is self-contained and may repeat some material from the previous chapter.

Demand is determined by relative price and real income. Income has a positive effect on demand while price has a negative effect on demand. This theory can be applied to explain the demand for non-durable goods and the demand for the consumption or the stock of durable goods too. Concerning the demand for a newly introduced durable good, my 1967 *American Economic Review* paper entitled "Technological change and the demand for computers" provided the following theory. I assumed that the change in the logarithm of annual demand is equal to a fraction *b* of the difference between the log of desired demand for the stock of the durable goods in equilibrium and logarithm of the existing stock. *b* measures the speed at which the log of the stock of new durable goods adjusts to its equilibrium level. Log equilibrium stock is a linear function of the log of relative and the log of real income.

The above theory assumes that *b* is constant through time. In this chapter, we generalize the above theory by allowing *b* to be time-varying. As a new product becomes mature, *b* might be increasing or decreasing.

I would add that when a new durable good is introduced, the price for a product of the same quality drops continuously. The decline in price is a measure of the rate of technology change. To illustrate this point, we consider the demand for new mainframe computers. Price is the price of a standard computer of a given quality. To measure quality, I computed an index composed of the speed of the computer, the size of its memory and its access time. To compute the weights of these three variables in the measurement of the quality of a computer, we can estimate a regression of price on these three characteristics for different computers in a given year. Using this measurement of quality, we find that the price of a computer of the same quality declines or the quality of computers of the same price improves through time. By such calculations, for example, if a computer costs US$1,000 in 2000, a computer of the same quality will cost much less in 2005. The percentage decline in price is a measure of technological change.

The US Department of Commerce Bureau of Census has applied the above method that I introduced in my 1967 *American Economic Review* paper to construct two price indices for non-portable computers and portable computers. Using 2002 as the base year, the average price of a non-portable computer of the same quality decreased from US$5,874 in 1993 to US$41 in 2001. The average price of a portable computer declined from US$10,089 in 1993 to US$39 in 2001. The rates of declines of the above two price indices are larger than the rates of decline of the average prices of these two types of computers being sold because the latter prices did not allow for technological improvement in the products being sold in different years. We divide the former price indices by the consumer price index to obtain the relative prices of the two types of computers. Similarly, we divide national income by the same consumer price index to obtain a measure of real income in the United States. All data used in this study are in Table 1.

In Chapter 17, we assumed b to be fixed, and estimated the price elasticity of demand for small US computers to be about 0.64, the income elasticity to be about 2.3 and the adjustment coefficient b to be about 0.64. Now assuming that b can change over time, we have found that from 1993 to 2011, b did not change substantially, with

Table 1. Personal Computers Data: 1993–2011.

Date	P_nonportable	P_port	Shipmt$	CPI	Income	P_avg	Purchase	Stock Y
1993	5873.7	10088.7	3253	78.679	6255.3	7138.2	0.455717	2.9757
1994	5198.2	8728	3951	80.302	6455.9	6257.14	0.631439	3.3096
1995	4184.6	6490.6	4878	82.079	6648.7	4876.4	1.000328	3.9790
1996	2895	4347.7	4935	83.864	6867.8	3330.81	1.481622	5.0627
1997	1951.4	2857.7	5525	85.434	7110.3	2313.92	2.387723	6.9441
1998	1165.6	1765.8	5572	86.246	7535.5	1405.68	3.963918	10.2136
1999	758.7	1024.4	5973	87.636	7763.5	864.98	6.905362	16.0976
2000	612.2	804.9	5775	89.819	8157.9	689.28	8.378308	22.8662
2001	431.8	540.6	4656	91.53	8356.3	475.32	9.795506	30.3751
2002	336	396	3978	92.778	8633.4	366	10.86885	38.2064
2003	268.9	299.8	3824	94.658	8850.5	284.35	13.44822	47.8340
2004	238.5	242.6	3420	97.121	9152.8	240.55	14.21742	57.2680
2005	178.4	188.2	3391	100	9277.4	183.3	18.49973	70.0409
2006	130.9	127.8	3533	102.723	9652.8	129.35	27.31349	90.3503
2007	97.9	97.1	3674	105.499	9880.3	97.5	37.68205	118.9973
2008	71	70.9	3789	108.943	10119.4	70.95	53.40381	160.5014
2009	54.6	55.8	2892	109.004	9883.3	55.2	52.3913	196.8426
2010	48.6	46.5	1640	111.087	10061.7	47.55	34.49001	211.6483
2011	40.7	39.2	1541	113.79	10183.6	39.95	38.57322	229.0567

its value moving between about 0.67 to about 0.70, while the estimates of price and income elasticity remain to be the same as in the case of a constant adjustment coefficient. Although in 2011 the product was in a more mature stage than in 1993 while innovations continued to take place, our model with a constant rate b of adjustment for log demand remains valid for the entire period with the same price and income elasticities.

In summary, we found that the theory of demand for a new product, as illustrated by the demand for mainframe computers from 1954 to 1965, can be used to explain the demand for small computers from 1993 to 2001. In addition, the theory that is based on a constant rate b for the logarithm of the stock of computers to adjust towards its equilibrium level can be applied in different stages of maturity of the new product. This research was conducted jointly with Professor Wang Peng of the Hong Kong University of Science and Technology.

Is the above theory of demand applicable in China? I believe so.

CHAPTER 19

What is the Future of China's Economy and Political System?

In this chapter, I will discuss three questions concerning China's economy and its political system in the next 10 to 15 years.

1. What will the rate of growth of GDP for China be in the next 10 to 15 years? This is the first question people will ask when discussing the future of the Chinese economy. My answer for the average rate of growth during this period will be about 8% or slightly higher, with the rate of growth in the first half of the period somewhat higher than in the second half. To justify my answer, I will point out that in the last three decades the growth rate averaged about 9.5%, remaining high even as late as 2008 to 2009 when there was a global recession in the US and Europe. The rate slowed down only slightly in 2011 and 2012. The three factors contributing to this rapid growth rate are:

(1) China has an abundance of high-quality human capital in the form of its resourceful entrepreneurs and hard-working and efficient workers, and an intelligent and reliable labor force in general. Such high-quality human capital has resulted from China's history and culture for thousands of years. During the Shang Dynasty, about 4,000 years ago, bronze vessels were made by high-quality labor using advanced technology.

(2) China has a set of functioning market institutions although some of these institutions are imperfect. During the period of central planning, China did not grow as rapidly because of the lack of this factor.

(3) As a latecomer, China has been able to catch up at a high speed. US possesses factors 1 and 2 but cannot grow rapidly because of the lack of factor 3.

China will continue to grow because the first two factors will remain unchanged while the force of the third factor will gradually decrease as China becomes more developed. The change of the third factor will be slow because China is a large country. While the coastal areas will become richer, much of the interior areas remain poor and will still provide much room for growth. That is why I gave the above prediction for the rate of growth in the next 15 years or so.

2. Concerning the development of China's political system, the ruling Communist Party will remain in power in the foreseeable future. Leaders of the Communist Party, like any ruling political leaders, are most interested in preserving their own power. In order to do so, the leaders have tried and will try to control the people in China, and provide them with what they desire if necessary. The leaders will use carrots and sticks. The carrots include social welfare, economic infrastructure, and social infrastructure such as the promotion of education and democracy. The promotion of democracy has been a topic included in the Annual Report of the Premier to the National People's Congress in recent years.

To complete my prediction of the future political system in China, besides the prediction of the political behavior of the leaders of the Communist Party, I would need to predict the reactions of the Chinese people to the policies of the Communist Party. Since the policies of the Communist Party are multi-dimensional and there are many segments of the Chinese population responding to the policies, the answer to the above question will depend on which policy and which segment of the population that we wish to predict. Even if we predict correctly the introduction of certain policies by the Communist Party in the future, we still need to predict which segments of the Chinese population will support these policies and which segments will not. Social stability in China will depend on how many segments of the Chinese population will strongly object to certain important policies in the future and whether the Communist Party of China will change these policies if there are strong objections to them.

After explaining the difficulties in predicting the future political developments of China, I can offer my judgment based on my understanding of the behavior of the Communist Party and of the Chinese people. In my opinion, the leaders of the Communist Party will be intelligent enough not to force unpopular policies on the Chinese people for the sake of their own survival and their desire to provide benefit to the Chinese people. Hence, China will be politically stable in the future.

The above statement is subject to one important reservation. I mentioned earlier that the political leaders in China are most concerned with the preservation of their political power. In addition, one should add that powerful political leaders are tempted to use their political power for personal gains. As a result, corruption is rampant in China, as recognized by the leadership of the Communist Party. The problem of corruption may be serious enough to affect the political stability of China but whether it will happen or not is difficult for me to predict.

3. Will a democratic government be developed in China? The answer depends on how democracy is defined. Some form of democracy will be developed gradually because both the Communist Party and the influential Chinese people desire it but the nature of China's democratic system will be different from the US system. In fact, even the democratic systems of the European countries are different from the US system. Note first that this topic is not as important for most of the people residing in China as for US intellectuals and the educated Chinese living in the US and Europe. When democracy is developed, its nature will be different from the form of democracy practiced in the US mainly because China has a different cultural tradition from the US. Americans value freedom while Chinese people value social order more. Americans are individualistic while the Chinese people are more community-minded. The Chinese value social harmony and law and order more than freedom. They are concerned with relations with members of their families, including their

elders and their friends. As a well-known essay on an ideal society with social harmony written by Confucius asserts, the wealth of the community is supposed to be shared by all, in contrast to the system of private property practiced in a Western democratic country, and people are supposed to take care of the children and elders of others as their own.

As far as the introduction of democracy is concerned, some form of elections may be introduced for the selection of officials in the government and of leaders of the Communist Party. At present, members of the Central Committee of the Communist Party are elected by representatives of the Party a level below. Members of the Political Bureau are elected by members of the Central Committee and members of the Standing Committee of the Political Bureau (the seven most powerful persons in China) are elected by members of the Political Bureau. At present, democracy is practiced in the form of direct election of village heads in many parts of China. In the future, direct election can be extended to the election of higher-level government officials.

CHAPTER 20

Further on the Future Growth Rate of China's Real GDP

In Chapter 19, I made a forecast of the growth of real GDP in China to be about 8% per year or slightly higher for the next 10 to 15 years. This optimistic forecast was based on observing the three fundamental factors contributing to China's high GDP growth, namely, abundance of high-quality human capital, a functioning market economy even if some market institutions are imperfect and the early stage of economic development which enabled China to leapfrog in its development. I reduced the projected growth rate from the rate of about 9.5% per year observed in the last three decades to only 8% because as China continues to grow, the third factor will be weakened.

However, some observers have claimed that the decades of hyper growth or double-digit GDP growth rate in China are gone. At the beginning of 2012, the Chinese premier set the goal of China's GDP growth rate at only 7.5%. At the 18th Party Congress in Beijing, the new Chinese leaders vowed to double both China's GDP and its GDP per capita in 10 years. To achieve this, China needs to maintain an average of GDP growth rate at only 7% for the coming decade.

Observers gave the following reasons for China to be able to achieve a 7% growth rate. First of all, savings rates are still very high. In addition, the Chinese government has generated large revenues every year to build infrastructure. Second, the literacy level remains high and the productivity continues to improve while the labor costs are still low. Third, regional disparity exists but the west and interior regions in China are expected to pick up in their development and catch up with the coastal provinces. Fourth, urban-rural disparity still exists. It was only recently that the urban dwellers reached over 50% of the population for the first time in China. Finally, China has remained underdeveloped in education, health services, and many other service industries. In comparison with many high-income and upper-middle-income countries, there is much for China to do in order to develop its service industries. Education and health services are among top priorities for the government to promote its sustainable development.

I cited the above reasons for China's fairly rapid growth to continue in the future because I recall that they were stated in the *New York Times*. The three factors that I gave above are fundamental factors, without which some of the factors cited in the *New York Times* would not exist.

In this chapter, I supplement my forecast of China's real GDP by using statistical methods to fit the logarithm of real GDP as a quadratic function of time. If the percentage rate of increase of real GDP is constant through time, the natural log of real GDP will be a linear function of time with a slope equal to the percentage rate of increase. If the percentage rate of increase has declined in recent years, the log of real GDP as a function of time will have a slope which is decreasing with time, as can be observed by fitting a quadratic function of time t for the log of real GDP and observing the coefficient of the square of time t to be negative. I have used official data for China's real GDP as found in the *China Statistical Yearbook* (Beijing: National Bureau of Statistics, 2012) and fitted such an equation. Denoting $t =$ year– 1978, the fitted equation using data from 1978 to 2011 is

$$\ln(\text{GDP}) = 7.617 + 0.093(.002)\, t + 0.000(.000)\, t^2 \quad R^2 = 1.00$$

where the number in parentheses after each coefficient is its standard error. The result is that the coefficient of the square of time is practically zero with an extremely small standard error. From the coefficient of t, we observe that the past growth rate of real GDP has been at an exponential rate of 0.93. The fitted line shows that the points for the observed log real GDP are close to a straight line. If this equation is projected forward for 10 to 15 years, the slope and thus the rate of increase in real GDP will remain constant and not decrease. Thus, simply by projecting past data on the logarithm of real GDP, we have found the rate of increase of real GDP to remain constant in the future. Such a forecast is more optimistic than my forecast of about 8% for China's GDP growth rate for the next 10 to 15 years. I have given the reasons for my forecast in Chapter 19 and as summarized above. The statistical analysis reported in this chapter supports my previous optimism which is derived from observing that the momentum of China's GDP growth seemed undiminished in recent years.

In conclusion, the undiminished rate of increase in China's real GDP as reported in this chapter lends further support for the forecast of 8% or slightly higher that I made in Chapter 19, which is considered by other observers to be too optimistic.

CHAPTER 21

Using Economic Models to Forecast China's Real GDP

In Chapter 20, I used a simple economic model to forecast China's real GDP. The model explains the natural log of GDP by a linear trend. In this chapter, a system of equations will be introduced to forecast real GDP.

There are three steps in using an econometric model to forecast. The first is to formulate a model based on economic theory. Often, this model consists of a system of equations. Second, the equations of the model are estimated by econometric method using the relevant economic data. This step involves statistical estimation and analysis. The third step is to project the estimated model forward in time to generate economic forecasts.

For the purpose of forecasting real GDP of China, I have chosen a model consisting of the following equations:

(1) A production function explaining the natural log of real GDP y as a linear function of the natural log of capital stock K and of labor L used to produce the output. In addition, time t is added as an additional variable. Its coefficient measures the change in total factor productivity, i.e., the increase in output even if the inputs capital stock and labor remain constant.

(2) An equation to explain the change of labor L through time. This is simply done by assuming that labor L increases by a constant percent per year as estimated by the data on the increase in L in recent years.

(3)   To project the increase in capital stock K in the future we use the equation

$$K(t) = 0.96\ K(t-1) + I(t)$$

where $K(t)$ is capital stock at the end of period t and $I(t)$ is gross investment during period t. In the above equation, the rate of depreciation of capital stock is 0.4 per year. This means that of the capital stock $K(t-1)$ at the end of last year, 0.96 remains this year.

(4)   To explain gross investment $I(t)$, we simply assume it to be a fraction of $y(t-1)$ and the fraction can be estimated by historical data.

Thus, the above model can be used to forecast y in the future if we know the production function (1).

I estimated the production described by (1) using the Chinese annual data from 1952 to 1998 as presented in Chapter 5 of my book, *China's Economic Transformation* (Wiley-Blackwell, 2007). For the purpose of making the forecast reported in this chapter, I have re-estimated the above production function using data up to 2011 and found the result very similar.

Using the above model to forecast the natural log of real GDP for 2012 to 2016, I have found its value to be 11.44, 11.54, 11.64, 11.74 and 11.84 respectively, beginning with an actual value of 11.34 for 2011. This means that the forecasts of five years are increasing at an exponential rate of 0.10 per year. This result is in agreement with the forecast by projecting the natural log or real GDP by a linear trend of time as done in a previous chapter.

However, my own forecast of real GDP for the next 10 to 15 years is lower, being at an annual rate of increase of 8% or slightly higher for reasons previously discussed. Economic forecasts are based on both judgment and quantitative analysis. Judgment is required because an econometric model may not be able to incorporate some of the important factors and it is constructed under the assumption that the same factors affecting the variables to be forecast will remain to be the most important factors in the future whereas new factors may appear in the future to affect the variable to be forecast. These new factors are not incorporated in an econometric model.

CHAPTER **22**

Efficient Stock Markets

Many people are interested in watching the movement of stock prices but it is very difficult to make money by buying and selling stocks. Naturally economists are also interested in the movement of stock prices and have made many studies about it but economists in general cannot make money from the stock market based on their studies. This chapter reports on how economists think about the movement of stock prices and how they explain why people cannot make money from trading in the stock market. This subject can be illustrated by the contributions of three economists who were awarded the Nobel Prize in 2013. The subject matter of this chapter is quite technical. Although I have tried my best to provide a clear exposition, it still requires much patience and effort for most readers to understand the content.

The first Nobel laureate, Eugene Fama of the University of Chicago studied and coined the term "efficient financial markets" in his article "Efficient capital markets: A review of theory and empirical work" that was published in the *Journal of Finance* in 1970. In an efficient financial market, no statistical model can be used to predict future stock prices to make money. The reason is that the current stock prices are determined by the information that the market participants already know. No one can know more than the market to make money by buying and selling stocks. Lars Hansen, also of the University of Chicago, contributed to statistical methods when rational expectations is assumed. This assumption can be used to construct economic models, including models for predicting stock market prices. I will explain the concept of rational expectations later in this chapter. Robert Shiller of Yale University compared the actual movements of stock prices with what economic theories predict and found that the actual prices moved more than what economic theory can predict.

It would be interesting (1) to study the movements of stock prices based on economic models under the assumption of rational expectations using methods proposed by Hansen and (2) to explain the movement of stock prices under the assumption that the prices already incorporated the information available to market participants as Fama would claim. Later we will discuss whether Shiller is correct to say that the actual movements are not satisfactorily explained by economic theory. The purpose of this chapter is to provide an example of (1) and (2) based on my study of stock market prices that was published as a paper entitled "Rational versus adaptive expectations in present value models" in the *Review of Economic and Statistics* in November 1989.

To perform the above two studies, we need to propose an economic model to explain stock prices. The proposed model is "the present value theory" of stock price. This theory asserts that the price of a stock today $p(t)$ is the sum of the discounted value of its expected future earnings $E[p(t+1) + d(t+1)]/(1+r)$. In the next period $t+1$ the owner of the stock can sell the stock to earn $p(t+1)$ and expect to receive a dividend $d(t+1)$. The two combined is his total future earnings. Since he does not yet know what this future earning will be, he takes its expected value $E[\ ]$. To convert this expected value to its present value we have to divide it by $(1+r)$ where r is the rate of interest. For example, if r is 0.05, the amount which I expect to receive next year has to be divided by 1.05 to convert it to the value for me today, or its "present value."

To perform study (1), I used statistical data to compare the actual prices of stocks $p(t)$ with the discounted sum of the expected values as explained above. The comparison requires estimating the expectation $E[\ ]$. This is done by using the concept of rational expectation. Rational expectation of a variable equals the mathematical expectation (mean) of that variable in the chosen econometric model. In study (1), I used the econometric models which were most commonly used to form mathematical expectations of $p(t+1)$ and $d(t+1)$. These econometric models explain $p(t+1)$ and $d(t+1)$ by linear functions of their past values. Using US annual data for the Standard and Poor's 500 stocks from 1871 to 1986, my study showed that the mathematical expectation $E[p(t+1) + d(t+1)]/(1+r)$ fails to explain $p(t)$ satisfactorily. This shows that although the assumption of rational expectations is a useful hypothesis for many applications, it may not be a good assumption for other applications. Thus, the important work of Hansen on rational expectations has its limitations like most works in economics.

To perform study (2), I needed to find some way to incorporate market information to form $E[p(t+1) + d(t+1)]/(1+r)$. One way to incorporate market information is to use the past data on $p(t) + d(t)$, denoted by $x(t)$, to form the expectation $E[x(t+1)] = E[p(t+1) + d(t+1)]$. This was done by using adaptive expectation as follows. Assume that people have an expectation equal to $Ex(t)$ and observe $x(t)$ in period t. To obtain a new expectation $Ex(t+1)$ for the next period $t+1$, people revise their expectation by using the formula $E[x(t+1)] = bx(t) + (1-b)Ex(t)$. Applying the formula for $x(t)$, we have $Ex(t) = bx(t-1) + (1-b)Ex(t-1)$. Substituting this formula for $Ex(t)$ in the previous equation and doing so repeatedly for $Ex(t-1)$, etc. we can use past data $x(t)$, $x(t-1)$,... to compute the expectation $E[x(t+1)]$ by adaptive expectations. This is how market participants can use available information to predict stock price $p(t) = E[x(t+1)]/[(1+r)]$. My study shows that such information can predict $p(t)$ very well. Thus the result is consistent with the efficient market hypothesis of Fama which states that stock price $p(t)$ is formed by the information available to market participants, namely $x(t)$, $x(t-1)$,.... Thus, econometric models such as the one described in the previous paragraph cannot beat the above model based on information available to market participants.

When Shiller points out that economic models do not explain all the fluctuations observed in historical data, he is correct to say that predictions of stock price based on any econometric model are always subject to error. Sometimes when the errors from using econometric models are large, he shows that the errors can be explained better by some psychological factors. He calls such psychological factors "irrational exuberance" which is the title of his popular book. It describes how people are driven emotionally and are excited to buy stocks when the stock prices rise rapidly, more so than economic theory can predict. This leads to large fluctuations in stock prices and even to a collapse in the stock market. "Irrational exuberance" described by Shiller is opposite to "rational expectations" assumed by Hansen and others.

In economics, although different contributions have different and even opposite points of view, they can all be considered important if they are original and useful. Furthermore, different economic discoveries can be likened to different parts of an elephant's body which are different.

CHAPTER 23

My Teacher Milton Friedman

In this chapter, I will first describe my experience as a student of Friedman's at the University of Chicago and then the topics in economics which are parts of his research and of my own that follow his up to his death in 2006. The main purpose of this chapter is to show how economic theory can be applied to understand and solve real-life economic problems. In my research there are two other areas not much affected by Friedman, one on econometric method and the second on dynamic economics as partly summarized in three books (*Econometrics* (New York: McGraw Hill, 1983); *Analysis and Control of Dynamic Economic Systems* (New York: John Wiley and Sons, 1975) and *Dynamic Economics* (Oxford University Press, 2007)).

1. Friedman as a Teacher at Chicago and the Chow Test

In 1951, I went to the University of Chicago to do graduate work and attended Friedman's class on price theory. When Friedman entered the classroom for his first class, he was impressive, more so than any other teacher that I had up to that time. His lectures were stimulating. At the first lecture he had already showed the power of economic theory for the understanding of the real world. His thinking process was sharp and he could react to statements by others almost immediately. In Chicago, I was also fortunate to be able to study under other great minds but Friedman had the most influence on me.

At the time when I was writing my thesis on the demand for automobiles in the United States with Al Harberger as adviser, I presented draft chapters to the Friedman Workshop on Money several times and received very useful comments from him. This was the workshop in which the Friedman-Meiselman work on comparing the usefulness of using the stock of money M as compared with autonomous expenditures A to explain national income Y. Regressions were performed by Meiselman to explain Y by A and Y by M and reported to the workshop. The regressions on M were found to have higher R-square. At one time of this workshop, Friedman had to distinguish between two definitions of M, with one including only currency and deposits and the second also including time deposits. Friedman remarked: "Let us call the first $M1$ and the second $M2$." I believe that this was how these familiar terms were invented.

Friedman suggested to me to use permanent income or expected income instead of current income to explain the demand for automobiles. Following his suggestion, I found his permanent income variable to be better in explaining the demand for the total stock of automobiles and current income to be better in explaining the annual purchases of automobiles. The reason is that annual purchase including savings which is influenced by current income. I will discuss the usefulness of permanent income in section 3. Friedman's introduction of the concept of permanent income or expected income also had a great influence on, if not marked the beginning of, the use of expectations in economics. He introduced the use of adaptive expectations which assumes that the annual change in expectations is a fraction of the difference between the observed value of the previous period and the expected value in the previous period. He used it to explain consumption and was awarded the Nobel Prize for this work. People had found that consumption increased less than current income proportionally. If so, the aggregate demand from consumption would be insufficient when current income increases, leading to depression without the intervention of government expenditures. Believing in the ability of capitalism with free markets to survive without government intervention, Friedman introduced permanent income to point out why consumption would increase proportionally with income and how economic growth in a free market economy will continue without government intervention.

2. Demand for Durable Goods

I learned from Friedman that past data can be explained by many hypotheses and therefore we can have confidence in a theory only if it can be used to predict observations in the future. This idea was used in my further work on the demand for automobiles in the US.

In 1958, my thesis adviser Al Harberger decided to publish a collection of PhD theses on the demand for durable goods which he advised after mine was completed. Since my thesis was already published in 1957, I had to write another paper for his volume. I decided to find out whether my demand equations estimated by using data up to 1953 could predict successfully data from 1954 to 1957. This was how the Chow test was invented to answer this question.

The accelerations principle used to explain a demand for the change in stock of a durable good by the change in income was based on the theory that the stock is dependent on income and therefore the rate of change is dependent on the rate of change in income. This principle was applied in my work on the demand for automobiles and was found to be valid later in many other works to explain the demand for other durable goods in the US, China and Taiwan.

3. Adaptive Expectations Versus Rational Expectations

As pointed out above, Friedman was responsible for bringing expectations to the forefront of economics and his formulation of expectations was adaptive expectations. Later, John Muth proposed another formulation known as rational expectations in his paper "Rational expectations and the theory of price movements" that was published in *Econometrica* in 1961. The latter equals the mathematical expectations of the variables as generated by the econometric models used by the econometrician. In this section, I will show why adaptive expectations can be better than rational expectations in explaining stock prices and long-term interest rates, and how aggregate consumption in Taiwan is better explained by an income variable based on adaptive expectations than by one based on rational expectations.

The first example is the use of the present value model to explain stock price by the expectation of the present value of future dividends and to explain a long-term interest rate by the expectation of a sum of discounted future short-term interest rates. Rational expectations failed in this case because no econometric models can predict future dividends and future interest rates successfully as pointed out in my article, "Rational versus adaptive expectations in present value models," in the *Review of Economics and Statistics* (1989). The article also shows adaptive expectations to be better in both cases.

In the second example, I studied aggregate consumption in China in a two-equation model of the Chinese macroeconomy ("National income determination in China," *Journal of Political Economy*, 1985; "A simple model of the Chinese macroeconomy," *Economic Letters*, 2010; and "Lessons from studying a simple macroeconomic model for China," *Economic Letters*, 2011) where the investment equation satisfies the accelerations principle, with investment explained by the rate of change in income and lagged investment and the consumption function explained by the permanent income hypothesis of Robert Hall ("Stochastic implications of the life cycle-permanent income hypothesis: Theory and evidence," *Journal of Political Economy*, 1987) under the hypothesis of rational expectations, with consumption explained by lagged consumption with coefficient equal to 1. Both equations are strongly supported by the Chinese annual data from 1952 to 2009 but for the data on Taiwan from 1951 to 2010, Friedman's expected income was better in explaining consumption while investment was successfully explained by the accelerations principle. One reason for rational expectations to fail is that the Taiwan government introduced a universal health care system in 1995 which changed the consumption function of our model.

After observing the research results reported above that are unfavorable to rational expectations, I became convinced that for most economics applications, adaptive expectations is a better hypothesis than rational expectations. My reasoning is based on the following two cases when an econometric model is proposed. First, the model is misspecified. In this case, there is no reason to assume that economic agents will use such a misspecified model to form mathematical expectations to represent their subjective expectations. Second, the model is correctly specified. In this case, it is unlikely that the economic agents know how to perform the complicated calculations to form mathematical expectations to represent their subjective expectations. To assume that they form their expectations as if they could perform such complicated calculations is a great leap of faith. In both cases, adaptive expectations may well be a simple rule for economic agents to form their subjective expectations of the variables of interest. Furthermore, there is much economic evidence supporting adaptive expectations since Friedman (1957). It is difficult to find empirical evidence to support or reject rational expectations because the assumption is imbedded in the application of complicated economic models, and particular deficiencies in a model are difficult to pinpoint. Such difficulties may be a reason why the assumption of rational expectations, though incorrect, is difficult for the faithful to give up.

4. The Demand for Money

Friedman's work has inspired research on the demand for money, including my own ("On the long-run and short-run demand for money," *Journal of Political Economy*, 1966). In that article, I explained demand equations for both the stock of money and the change in the demand annually following the methodology of my work on the demand for automobiles. Long-run demand for stock of money depends on income and the rate of interest. Short-run demand was based on a stock adjustment model where the flow, annual change, is a fraction of the difference between the desired stock as determined by the former model and the observed stock. The article received much attention as there were many comments published later in the same journal.

5. Inflation and the Effects of Money Supply on Price and Output.

On inflation, I began with the quantity theory of money which Friedman had taught me, namely, the quantity equation, $Mv=PY$, where M is money supply, P is a price index and Y is national output. The equation becomes a theory if the change in velocity v is empirically small. Following this idea in my study of inflation, I started with the equation $\ln P = \ln v + \ln(M/Y)$. This suggests that the most important variable explaining $\ln P$ is $\ln(M/Y)$. To explain inflation in China, I used Chinese data to estimate a regression to explain $\ln P$ by $\ln(M/Y)$ successively ("Money and price determination in China," *Journal of Comparative Economics*, 1987). As inflation is defined as $\ln P(t) - \ln P(t-1) = \Delta \ln P(t)$ I used three variables to explain it: $\Delta \ln(M/Y)$, $\Delta P(t-1)$ of the last period to show a delayed effect, and the residual of the regression of $\ln P$ on $\ln(M/Y)$ in the last period. The last variable is known as the error correction term, since the regression of $\ln P$ on $\ln(M/Y)$ shows an equilibrium relation between these variables and its residual is a deviation from the equilibrium level. In the following period, the residual will have a negative effect on inflation. This equation was first estimated in 1985 at the request of the then Chinese Premier Zhao Zhiyang who was concerned about inflation because money supply M had increased by 50% in 1984. I later reported to the Premier that according to my equation, inflation in 1985 would only be moderate, most likely to be under 9%. Later in 1986–1988, money supply increased by about 30% per year. The result was serious inflation in 1989 which was an important cause, in addition to corruption, for the Tiananmen Incident in 1989.

In later studies of inflation in China, I updated this study and found that the above equation to explain inflation remained to be valid (Chow and Peng Wang, "The empirics of inflation in China," *Economic Letters*, 2010). I separated the regression for inflation in China into two periods, one using data up to 1978 and the other beginning from 1979 as economic reform started at that time. The amazing result was that the coefficients of the two regressions were almost identical, with the Chow test showing a small F statistic corresponding to a critical value of about 0.5. Thus, the same equation explaining inflation in China is valid during the period of planning and when China became a market economy. Although the government tried to control the prices of some commodities during the period of planning, inflation was still affected by the changed M/Y. As an example, the price level increased by 16% in 1961 when M increased slowly but total output decreased by over 30% as a result of the Great Leap Forward Movement of 1958–1961.

6. The Effect of an Exogenous Change in Money Supply on Output and the Price Level

I attended a conference to honor Milton and Rose Friedman as authors of the book *Free to Choose* organized by the Federal Reserve Bank of Dallas during October 23–24, 2003. In that conference, Ben Bernanke presented a paper providing evidence from works of his own on the Friedman proposition concerning the effects of an exogenous change in money supply on aggregate output and the price level. The proposition states that effect on the former is immediate but only temporarily and the effect on the latter is delayed but long-lasting. I was interested in this proposition and wanted to find out whether it would be valid for China. When I told Friedman about my intended study he stated confidently, "My proposition will be valid for China" while I was not sure.

To test the Friedman proposition, I estimated a second order VAR model for $\log P$, $\log Y$ and $\log M$ as the three variables. This study (Chow and Shen Yen, "Money, price level and output in the Chinese macroeconomy," *Asia-Pacific Journal of Accounting and Economics*, 2005) is too technical to be reported here. When I reported the result to Friedman, he was pleased but not surprised to find that his proposition on the effects of an exogenous change in money supply on output and price is valid for China.

7. Friedman on China

Friedman visited China in 1988 when he met with the then Secretary General (formerly Premier) Zhao Zhiyang. After the meeting, both expressed respect for the other. After the Tiananmen Incident in 1989, Friedman was predicting economic collapse in China, including serious inflation and reduction in the growth of national income. These views were expressed in his article published in *San Francisco Chronicle* on June 22, 1989. Later, in June 1989, I made a speech in Hong Kong to a group of Princeton alumni, which was later published in *Princeton Alumni Weekly*, September 27, 1989, stating that the effect of the Tiananmen Incident would have only a limited effect on China's GDP with a total effect of about 5 percentage points in the five years after 1989 because economic growth was driven mainly by economic forces which were strong in the case of China at that time. Soon after my forecast turned out to be correct, I wrote to Friedman pointing out his error as expressed in the above article. He returned my email by saying that he should not have expressed a strong opinion on a subject about which he had only limited knowledge. However, he made the same mistake later when he predicted that after Hong Kong was returned to China in 1997 it would be impossible to maintain the currency of Hong Kong separately because there could not be two currencies in one country while Deng Xiaoping was implementing the policy of "one country two systems" for Hong Kong.

Friedman has a high regard for economic freedom as shown by his authorship with Rose Friedman of the book *Free to Choose*. In the conference organized by the Federal Reserve Bank of Dallas in October 2003 where the book was honored, Friedman recommended my participation at the conference by way of presenting a paper related to it. The result was my article "Free to choose in China" that discusses the eight topics in the book as being practiced in China – (1) Economic freedom, (2) Relation between economic and political freedom, (3) Role of the government, (4) Social welfare, (5) Education, (6) Protecting the consumer, (7) Macroeconomic policy and (8) Trend toward more freedom, which was published in the conference volume edited by Mark A. Wynne, Harvey Rosenblum and Robert L. Formainai, *The Legacy of Milton and Rose Friedman's Free to Choose: Economic Liberalism at the Turn of the 21st Century* (Dallas, Texas: Federal Reserve Bank of Dallas, 2004, pp. 153–71).

8. Effect on my View of the World and my Attitude in Life

One aspect of the ideas expounded in *Free to Choose* is Friedman's faith in the free market to solve almost all economic problems. When I graduated from the University of Chicago, I held the same viewpoint. My viewpoint began to change after I started teaching at the Sloan School of Management at Massachusetts Institute of Technology (MIT). My view about the efficiency of the free market was affected by the MIT environment. During the first semester at MIT, I was invited by Jan Tinbergen to have lunch at the Harvard Faculty Club as Tinbergen was visiting Harvard University. Tinbergen wanted to see me to discuss the possible publication of my thesis as a volume of the series, *Contributions to Economic Analysis*, of which he was chief editor. Knowing my interest in the demand for automobiles, he mentioned to me his idea to export American used cars to Europe where there was a short supply of automobiles. My immediate reaction was "If there is a need to ship American cars to Europe, the market would have done it." After hearing my comment, Tinbergen replied "That was just a thought." That remark embarrassed me and led me to reflect on the efficiency of the market.

At MIT when I was exposed to the views of Paul Samuelson and Robert Solow, I began to think of the role of the government in the economy, in addition to other aspects of economics not taught in Chicago. Keynesian economists believe in the effectiveness of government expenditures in periods of recession. Even in the use of monetary policy there is the distinction of using rules versus discretion with Friedman advocating the rule of a constant increase in money supply while others would adjust money supply depending on the state of the macroeconomy. Let me provide some examples of what I consider to be the limitation of the market and the role of the government.

In the case of the development of new industries in a developing economy, the government seems to have an important role. According to the Chicago School, it is not the role of the government to establish enterprises or even to pick the winners among private enterprises in the course of economic development. My experience as an economic adviser to the government of Taiwan from the 1960s to the late 1970s has convinced me otherwise. I observed many economic officials in the government to be very intelligent and to know which industries to support and which industries or firms to promote. The role of Dr. K.T. Li, then Minister of Economic Affairs, is an outstanding example. I was able to observe that the government could do a great deal and that leaving the job of economic development entirely to the free market would not have worked as well. As an example, the Taiwan government established the Industrial Technology Research Institute (ITRI) in 1973 to engage in applied research and technical services that originated in Taiwan. ITRI not only helped selected industries through the provision of particular technological knowhow but also helped establish particular private enterprises including the Taiwan Semiconductor Manufacturing Company that was founded and led by Dr. Morris Chang.

As I observe the Chinese economy today, the government is active in establishing and operating state-owned enterprises. At the same time, it has allowed the entry of private enterprises to compete with the state enterprises. My own view is that while private enterprises should be encouraged, one should not rule out the establishment and operation of state-owned enterprises as long as the two types of enterprises can compete in a level playing field. To prevent either type of enterprises from operation would only reduce competition in production, distribution and the development of new technology.

Intellectually, Friedman has taught me how to think clearly and how to seize the crux of a problem and to formulate a simple hypothesis to explain a seemingly complicated problem. On a personal level, Friedman has taught me to develop self-confidence and self-respect. Friedman did not treat people of high positions or celebrities in general differently from ordinary people. To him all men indeed are created equal. As I recall, Alan Greenspan once remarked, Friedman would speak to a US president with the same demeanor as to a college student. I have learned this attitude from him in my own dealing with different types of people. On the other hand, I seemed to have observed Friedman's insistence on his viewpoint, perhaps including his referee report on my paper on the demand for money. If so, this taught me to be more open-minded and more willing to consider opposite views of others. Friedman had the ability to apply economic knowledge to make appropriate policy recommendations. In addition, his ideas have led to social change without him serving as a government official. He influenced the formulation of government policies by spreading his ideas in books, by training students, by lecturing and by presenting his ideas based on his book *Free to Choose* on TV.

He has influenced so many people who will carry on his ideas for years to come. We all miss him greatly.

PART 3

Economic Policy

CHAPTER 24

From Economic Theory to Economic Policy Analysis

Good academic economists often do not know how to give good policy advice. When they leave the ivory tower to serve as advisors to the government, many begin to realize their shortcoming in this regard. How can economic theory be successfully applied to the formation of good economic policy? I will try to answer this question by providing some personal experiences in advising China's government in its market reform during the last 30 years as recorded in a television interview conducted by *Diyi Caijing Daily* or "First Financial Daily" in English. Other topics are also covered below.

1. The Necessity of Price Reform

"First Financial Daily": As an experienced economist, what do you think about China's reform and opening up during the last 30 years?

Chow: China's reform from a planned economy to a market economy was not easy to accomplish. In 1953, China started its first five-year plan. Many people accepted the idea of planning. To change the belief in planning to accepting the operation of market economy was not easy. I admire Deng Xiaoping for believing that the change was correct and for guiding the change. To direct the Chinese people to change, he advised, "Cross the river by feeling the stones." That is to say, based on the experience of reform, take the next step forward.

"First Financial Daily": You just mentioned that the reform should be gradual and be carried out step by step. As far as I know, you also participated in the decision-making of the reform process. Can you tell us the story of your participation?

Chow: Price reform was the most important step, as I related to the Chinese Premier in 1984 during our first meeting. Just giving autonomy to state-owned enterprises was not enough because the decisions of these enterprises would not be economically efficient unless the enterprises are guided by market determined prices. If we do not let the market forces of supply and demand determine prices, economic resources would be misallocated. At the time the prices of many inputs supplied to state enterprises were set too low, leading to misuse of these resources. Also the price of housing was very low when workers paid only a few yuan for their monthly rental. Another example was the foreign exchange rate of the RMB, leading to the low official price of the US dollar. This created a shortage of the dollar, requiring special permits to buy the dollar for the import of foreign goods. All these prices should be set by the market forces of demand and supply to achieve efficient allocation of resources.

"First Financial Daily": Reform began in the agricultural sector under the household responsibility system. This reform was very successful. Why?

Chow: According to economic theory, optimum output should be determined by setting marginal revenue equal to marginal cost. If the producer is required to pay a fixed cost, his marginal calculation will not be affected. The household responsibility system amounts to charging the farm household a fixed amount of their output and leaving the rest for its own use. The farm household could treat this as a fixed cost which did not affect the optimum output it produced.

Under the commune system, if a farmer tried to work hard to increase the output of the work team he did not get the increased output because it would be shared by all members of the team. Under the household responsibility system, if a farm family works harder it gets all the increased output after paying a fixed amount as tax. Therefore, it has the right incentive to produce more.

"First Financial Daily": We found that the contract responsibility system was not equally successful when applied to different areas. For example, when applied to state-owned enterprises it was not as successful whereas in rural areas, it was completely successful. Why?

Chow: If enterprises did not pay for more work, workers would not have the incentive to produce more. Also the salaries of managers were set too low, discouraging them to apply their best effort. When enterprises made profits, parts of the profits were spent to purchase durable goods like refrigerators and TV sets for distribution to the workers and managers.

Township and village enterprises (TVEs) had higher productivity than state-owned enterprises because they paid higher salaries to managers and higher wages to workers. Salaries of TVEs managers were about two to three times those of state enterprise managers.

2. Increase in Money Supply and Inflation

"First Financial Daily": Reviewing the past years of experience in the reform, we found that in the implementation of the reform process, much inflation has occurred. Today, we are also facing inflationary pressures. You participated in the fighting of inflation in the late 1980s. How should we deal with inflation today? Two years ago, you mentioned that there would be inflation in China in the coming years.

Chow: I have studied China's inflation since 1985. I came to China in 1985 to organize a summer course in economics. At that time, China's leaders attached great importance to the issue of inflation. In 1984, the currency in circulation in China had increased by 50%. The Premier was much concerned about possible inflation in 1985 and asked me to study the situation. I formulated an econometric model to explain inflation and estimated the parameters of the model using data from 1952 to 1984. The most important variable to explain inflation is money supply in relation to national output. Inflation is caused mainly by the rapid increase in money supply, with delayed effects. Professor Milton Friedman has established a proposition about the effects of an increase in money supply. The immediate effect is to increase output but the effect would be short-lived.

Otherwise, we can promote economic growth simply by increasing the supply of money. The delayed effect is to increase the price level. This effect is permanent.

"First Financial Daily": Long-term economic growth would not be affected?

Chow: Correct. However, the impact on prices will be slower to appear, perhaps in one to two years. In 2002, the Chinese currency increased rapidly. Why? One important reason was that the yuan was undervalued, leading to increase in Chinese exports and the accumulation of a large amount of foreign reserves. The foreign reserves were converted to RMB. It was difficult for the People's Bank to prevent such an increase in money supply. We can observe the rapid increase in money supply in 2002, 2003 and 2004. Therefore, I predicted two years ago that inflation would come in about two years later.

"First Financial Daily": Some people think that the inflation now is cost-push inflation. In the late 1980s, inflation might have been the result of increase in demand. What do you think?

Chow: In the fall of 1988, prices increased at an annual rate of about 30%. In March 1989, members of the Commission for the Reconstruction of the Economic System met in Hong Kong mainly to discuss how to solve the inflation problem. I was an adviser to this Commission and invited Professor S. C. Tsiang of Cornell University (who was also the chief economic adviser to the Taiwan government) and Professor Lawrence Lau of Stanford University to participate. After the discussion, we believed that the most effective solution to reduce inflation was to raise interest rates. Because inflation was caused by a large amount of money in the hands of the people who were spending it and spending would raise prices, raising the interest rate would encourage people to deposit more money in the banks. We recommended raising the interest rate to about 12% so that the depositors would earn a positive real rate of return after adjusting for the increase in prices. The recommendation was accepted and inflation soon stopped.

I believe that the current inflation is also caused by the rapid increase in money supply. If we allow the yuan to appreciate, our trade surplus would be reduced and the inflow of foreign exchange would be reduced. The supply of money would accordingly be increasing more slowly to slow down inflation. The inflation problem would be solved.

3. From Academic Economic Research to the Formulation of Economic Policy

"First Financial Daily": You have contributed a great deal in promoting economics education in China and in advising the government on economic reform and the open door policy. Could you tell us something about your work in this regard?.

Chow: On education, I feel greatly honored to have the opportunity to offer my assistance. In 1980, I was one of the lecturers to lecture on econometrics to a group of about 100 Chinese scholars in the Summer Palace in Beijing. Later in 1983, the Ministry of Education sent a delegation to the United States to get help to improve legal and economics education in China — Mr. Wang Zenong was responsible for developing these two fields and Mr. Wang Fu Sun was the Foreign Affairs Officer. On October 23, they came to see me at my home in Princeton seeking my help in the field of economics. I was surprised and delighted by their interest. I offered to organize three summer workshops on microeconomics, macroeconomics and econometrics respectively in the summers of 1984, 1985 and 1986. The first workshop took place in Peking University and the other two in Renmin University. From 1985 to 1995, I helped organize a year-long workshop in economics at Renmin University, and from 1988 to 1993, another annual workshop at Fudan University. These were called the "Ford classes" because financial support was provided by the Ford Foundation. The Commission on Education, now the Ministry of Education, designated representatives from seven major universities to form a Committee on Economics Exchange with the United States, chaired by the then Vice President and later President Huang Da of Renmin University. The Ford Foundation designated Professor Dwight Perkins of Harvard University and me as the two co-chairmen of the Committee on Education and Research in Economics to work with the Chinese Committee. These two committees met annually, alternating between China and the United States. After 1996, the Ford Foundation did not continue its sponsorship because the Foundation does not sponsor a single activity for a long period.

I also cooperated with the Education Commission to select a group of the best graduate students in China every year to pursue a PhD degree in economics in the best American and Canadian universities. I provided examination questions in economics while the Education Commission provided examination questions in mathematics to select the students. This program was known as the Chow program and the examination was known as the "Chow test" after another Chow test used in statistics which I developed in 1960. Now these students are very accomplished, working in China or in the United States. I admire the talents of these young Chinese who were brought up in the Chinese culture that instils good working habits and they were also selected from a very large population.

"First Financial Daily": You wrote a very interesting article, suggesting that good academic economists may not be able to offer good advice on economic policy. Can you provide some examples of your statement?

Chow: Many people know economic theory well and have published important papers in top economics journals. However, when they are presented with a real-life economic problem, they may not know which economic tools to select to solve the problem. Let me provide two examples. In the first example, from 1997 to 1999, there was an Asian financial crisis. The International Monetary Fund sent economists to Asian countries to recommend solutions. The economists are very distinguished academic economists, but they diagnosed the problems incorrectly. When there was a need to conduct expansionary macroeconomic policies, they recommended contracting government expenditures, which was opposite to the correct policy. They are very respectable economists. Some countries following their recommendations were ruined economically.

As another example, there was a very well-known economist in the United States, serving as an undersecretary of an important department of the US government, who was providing economic advice to some African countries. Drawing from the economic principle that development of human capital is important for economic development, he recommended the solution of improving elementary and high school education for some African countries. His recommendation was not feasible because without sufficient human capital, these countries do not have enough qualified school teachers in the first place. One day he came to talk to me, I said I agreed with him that human resources are very important, but in Africa the problem is how to develop human capital when these countries do not have the human capital in the first place. There are not enough school teachers to educate the students.

"First Financial Daily": We also found that even when there is a good policy proposal, the timing to recommend or to introduce it is very important. If the timing is missed, one may miss the opportunity to propose an economic reform. It would be unproductive if the proposal is made too early when the conditions are not ripe. In this regard, what is your personal experience?

Chow: Timing is indeed very important. In addition, in discussing economic issues with policy makers, one should first consider whether the policy implementation is feasible.

4. Economics of Health Care and of Environmental Protection

"First Financial Daily": You recently developed some interest in the economics of health care provision and of the environment. In these areas, both economic theory and good policy recommendations are required. Could you tell us some of your ideas concerning these two areas?

Chow: Economic theory can be applied in many areas, such as health care. Today I went to a hospital for treatment using Chinese medicine. People say a doctor's service is hard to obtain and is very expensive.

I teach a course on China's economy. During the course of China's rapid economic development, consumption of all consumer goods and services increased rapidly except for health care. Statistics show that the per capital supply of health care did not increase from the early 1990s to the 2000s, as measured by the number of doctors, the number of medical personnel in general and the number of hospital beds per 10,000 of the Chinese population.

"First Financial Daily": Supply has not increased when people's income are increasing?

Chow: Yes. Why did the supply fail to increase? I think the most important reason is that the supply of health care is the responsibility of the government. The central government delegated this responsibility to the local governments. The financial resources of the local governments are limited. They choose to use them for urban development while providing just enough health care to the population. In fact, the solution is very simple: the central authorities should encourage more private hospitals to be established all over China. This policy does not require a large amount of government expenditure like the policy for Western Development, but only a policy announcement. The announcement will increase competition in the supply of health care leading to an increase in quantity and an improvement in quality of health care supply.

"First Financial Daily": Well, in the field of environment protection, what would you suggest to protect the environment while promoting economic development?

Chow: On water and air pollution, caused in part by industrial production, one policy is to control the pollution. A better approach is to allow it but to require the polluter to pay for the cost of pollution to society. On how much to pay, we should let the State Environmental Protection Department issue licenses available to all polluters. There are two problems to be resolved. First, how much should a polluter pay for each license or permit? Second, what is the number of permits to be issued within a region? Given answers to these two questions, polluters are allowed to trade the permits at market prices, or prices as mutually agreed upon. The total number of permits can be determined by surveying the opinions of the residents in ways that I have discussed in my writings.

5. Optimal Control and Macroeconomic Policies

"First Financial Daily": In econometrics, the Chow test is now a very popular tool. How did you discover this test?

Chow: I wrote a doctoral dissertation at the University of Chicago on the demand for automobiles in the United States. I estimated a demand function for automobiles, an equation that explains the number of cars to be sold. There are two important variables in the demand equation. One is the price of automobiles. The lower the car prices, the larger the number of cars that the US consumers would wish to buy. The second is income. The higher their income, the more the consumers would wish to buy. I completed my dissertation in 1955, having used annual data from 1921 to 1953 to estimate the demand equation. Note that in 1921, the cars in the US were very different from those produced in the early 1950s and yet the same demand equation could explain the demand for automobiles for the entire period. In 1958, I wanted to find out whether my demand equation remained valid in explaining the demand for cars from 1954 to 1957. The Chow test was used to test statistically whether the observations from 1954 to 1957 came from the same equation as those from 1921 to 1953. It could be used to find out whether the new observations are consistent with the estimated equation even when these observations are not sufficient to estimate a separate regression. I published the above test in an article in *Econometrica* in 1960.

"First Financial Daily": Do you think that optimal control can be used to determine good macroeconomic policies? But we also learned the Lucas critique which raised doubt about the usefulness of optimal control in the above application. You do not agree with this. Can you tell us your opinion?

Chow: Yes. I became interested in this topic while I was doing research at the IBM Thomas J. Watson Research Center from 1962 to 1970. While working on econometrics, I began to study the US macroeconomy and built a macroeconomic model for the United States. Later, I wanted to find out whether such a macroeconomic model can be used in the formation of an economic policy. Assuming different policies, one can use the model to determine the time paths of economic variables generated by the macro-model. To go one step further, one can use some tools to choose among these time paths and decide which policy is the best. This is done using the method of optimal control. After my research, the topic of optimal control for the determination of macroeconomic policy became a very popular topic in macroeconomic research not only in the US but also in Europe and Japan.

In the 1970s when I became a professor at Princeton, Robert Lucas wrote an important article, "Macroeconomic policy evaluation: A critique." This article suggests that it is inappropriate to use optimal control to determine desirable macroeconomic policies because when the policy changes, the parameters of the macroeconomic model will also change, making the predictions based on different policies invalid. I questioned this critique because in practice there would be only very small changes in the model parameters when different policies are applied. By how much the parameters will change depends partly on the behavior of the economic agents. If the agents are rational in the sense of incorporating the policy change into their behavior as described by the model equations, the parameters of these equations might change. The Lucas proposition may not be valid. Assuming that the economic agents are rational, their behavior as described by econometric equations in the model may not change. Take the example of the demand equations for automobiles. Changes in prices and income would affect the quantity demanded. If the government increases the excise tax on the purchase of automobiles, the price that consumers pay for automobiles will change but the demand equation itself will not change. As another example, if the Federal Reserve raises the interest rate, the demand for money equation may not change. The amount of money will decrease according to the demand equation that the economists have estimated.

6. Sustainable Economic Growth for China

"First Financial Daily": In the reform and opening up during the last 30 years, you have played an important role. Can you share with us some of your experience in this regard?

Chow: Let me discuss two aspects. One is foreign investment and the other is foreign trade. Attracting foreign investment has allowed China to import foreign capital, foreign technology and foreign management system into China, thus benefiting China's economic growth. Foreign trade made it possible for China to import materials and consumer goods that China cannot produce efficiently and it also allows China to export its products to earn foreign exchange to pay for its imports and to increase the demand for its outputs and thus increase its national product. China is now developing its economy through exports. Under the open door policy, Chinese students can go abroad to study. When they return to China, human capital in China will increase. Therefore, the open door policy was very important for China's economic development.

"First Financial Daily": About the prospects of China's future economic growth, people have different opinions. Some people think that rapid growth will continue for 30 years. Others think only about 10 to 15 years. What do you think?

Chow: You just raised two questions. One is the prospect of continued economic reform. The other is the continuation of economic growth. These are two different questions. Talking about market reform, the prospect is that it will be slow, partly because much reform has been completed and economic institutions change slowly. But growth can be rapid without much further reform. You asked me earlier about the growth rate. I think there are three important factors accounting for the rate of economic growth. The first is the existence of market institutions. China has a market economy, although market reform is not yet complete and there are institutional shortcomings. The factor of having a sufficient set of market institutions will continue. The second factor is human capital, i.e. the quality of the

Chinese people, farmers, workers, entrepreneurs, teachers, researchers, etc. China has an abundance of high-quality human capital. This is an important factor for China's economic growth. The third growth factor is the degree of economic development or how far China is behind the most developed countries, that is, the technology gap between China and the most advanced countries. The US has the first two factors but not the third. Therefore, the rate of its economic growth is slow. For China, to the extent that these three factors continue to operate, its economic growth will persist. In my opinion, there is still much room for China to grow fairly rapidly for some time, say, at the rate of about 8% in the next 15 years or so.

"First Financial Daily": So after 15 years, it might be a little bit slower?

Chow: A little slower. It may be 7% or 6%.

Source: First Financial Daily — http://www.aisixiang.com/data/30679.html.

CHAPTER 25

China's Foreign Policies in the Midst of the World Recession

Recently, I attended a public lecture at Princeton University, entitled "The United States after the financial crisis and China's foreign policy." The speaker is a well-known professor of the Woodrow Wilson School of Public and International Affairs. He had just returned to Princeton from diplomatic service for the United States government. At the time, the prominent news included China's tough stand in dealing with the Japanese government after the Chinese fishing boat was returned to China and the conflict with Vietnam and other neighboring countries over territorial waters in the South China Sea.

The speaker believes that as one of the world's major powers, China is still inexperienced in dealing with diplomatic affairs. China's economy has been growing so rapidly that many government officials are still not prepared to deal with challenging problems in diplomatic relations. China's foreign policy is handled by different government departments and is in need of coordination and strong leadership. As a new leader of the world, China needs to continue to improve its diplomatic skills.

China pursues the "equal treatment for all countries" as a major objective of its foreign policy. It wants to help other developing countries as much as possible. Such principles have been recognized and appreciated around the developing world. By contrast, the US government has shown its attitude to act as a big brother towards many smaller countries and a strong desire to use them to implement its own policies. Someone asked, in this recession, would China as a leader be able to introduce any policy to help out? Given China's current economic strength and resources, one would ask whether China would know how to use its resources effectively to help other countries.

I believe that China can help Europe out of the debt crisis. China holds 3 trillion dollars in foreign exchange reserves, of which about 400 billion dollars is in US Treasury bonds. Part of the money can be used to help solve the debt problem in some countries by providing them with loans. But in any case, China still needs to guard itself against the possibility of default. This can be done by requiring the borrowing countries to provide certain assets as collateral, such as natural resources and the right to develop these resources. In addition, the borrowing country can also use real estate, tax revenue and future income as guarantee.

I suggest that the Chinese government should increase the imports of US goods, which will not only benefit the Chinese consumers, but also provide capital goods and technology to develop western China. As one of the leaders of the world, China should employ its economic resources not only for national self-interests, but also for the benefit of the world. From this perspective, China has many opportunities, but the government needs to plan carefully to fulfill its duties.

In the formulation of foreign policy, there are some important considerations. First, the United States and other major European countries, and even some countries in need of financial assistance, may be envious of China's economic strength and hesitate to receive China's assistance. Second, China should lend a helping hand only if a country asks for help.

Evaluation of the Policy to Reform the Economic System in China

According to an article in the *New York Times* dated May 25, 2013, the Chinese government is planning to allow private businesses and market forces to play a larger role in the economy. This new policy is intended to improve living conditions for the middle class and to make China an even stronger competitor on the global stage. In a speech to party cadres, the country's new Prime Minister Li Keqiang said in May that the central government would reduce the state's role in economic matters in order to unleash the creative energies of a nation. This includes giving competition among private businesses a bigger role in investment decisions and setting prices. According to a directive issued on the government's website, the broad proposals include a tax on natural resources (in order to reduce the use of natural sources which are limited in supply and to reduce pollution when such resources are used), taking gradual steps to allow market forces to determine bank interest rates and developing policies to promote the entry of private capital into finance, energy, railways, telecommunications and other areas. Foreign investors will be given more opportunities to invest in banking, finance, logistics, heath care and other sectors. The policy directives also include loosening foreign exchange controls, and allowing the market to determine the value of the Chinese currency, the renminbi.

Observers believe that, in spite of the above market reforms, the government is unlikely to break up huge state-run oligopolies or privatize major sectors of the economy which the government considers to be strategic, such as banking, energy and telecommunications. Observers also believe that the major reason for the change to market-oriented policy is because the economy has slowed down as a result of fewer exports to Europe and the United States and slower investment growth. Rising labor costs and a strengthening currency have also reduced manufacturing competitiveness. Another factor for adopting the abovementioned reforms is that the Chinese population is aging and the number of young people entering the labor force has begun to decline, forcing China to upgrade its industrial operations and to compete using something other than inexpensive goods and low-cost labor.

Let me first point out that in the last two decades, rapid economic growth in China was mainly the result of the energy and resourcefulness of Chinese private entrepreneurs. This fact was recognized when the new policies were announced. In addition, I would like to make three sets of comments on the new policies.

First, the introduction of market-oriented policies is not new but follows a tradition which started when market reform started in 1978. State-run collective farms under the communes were replaced by private farming under the household responsibility system. State-run enterprises were first given autonomy in output decisions and were later replaced by corporations owned by stock holders in the late 1990s under the principle of allowing small enterprises to be privatized while the government was still holding on to the large and strategic ones, 爬大放小, a principle that was stated again in the current policy of extending market forces. Reducing the state control of market prices began in 1984 and is now a part of the current economic reform. For the banking system, commercial banks were established in a new banking system under the direction and supervision of the central bank, and now under the new directives the commercial banks would be given more discretion in the setting of interest rates. The setting of a more flexible exchange rate began in 1996 when the renmenbi was revalued, followed by a policy towards a more flexible exchange rate to be determined by market forces. Since China's entry into the World Trade Organization (WTO) in

2001, tariffs on agriculture and industrial products were supposed to be reduced step by step and foreign investment was allowed to enter the sectors of banking, finance and service industries in general. This policy was restated in the new directives mentioned above. In other words, the new policies are either extensions of past policies or are a way of allowing the announced past policies to be materialized.

Second, on the contents of the new policies, one may ask whether each new policy that allows the market to operate is appropriate and whether there may be other sectors which should be opened to market competition. My answer is that in all sectors of the economy, including those not mentioned in the first paragraph, private firms should be allowed to enter. Let competition decide which firm, public or private, old or new, should exist. There is no rationale for holding certain strategic sectors to be controlled by the government alone. If the government considers a certain sector to be important or strategic, it can establish and run its enterprises to make sure that the functions of that sector are performed. In the meantime, it should also allow private business to enter because in doing so, competition will make the government enterprises in the sector more efficient and the private firms will strengthen that sector. It is encouraging to learn from the *New York Times* article that health care is one of the sectors that would allow private business to enter. This became the government policy only about three years ago while before that, only public hospitals were allowed to function. The former policy was responsible for "看病贵" and allowing private hospitals to enter would increase the supply, improve the quality and lower the price of health care. Furthermore, allowing private firms to engage in all economic activities may lead to the establishment of a new sector in the economy or a new set of institutions being opened up by these firms. For example, the New York Stock exchange was not established by the government like the exchanges in Shanghai and Shenzhen. Seeing the need to trade stocks, the private sector established the New York Stock Exchange. In the 1930s, China also had a stock market established by the private sector. In general, there will be private investments in a new economic sector when the conditions require. If such private investment fails, it means that such a sector is not economically sustainable. If such private invest-ment succeeds, there is no need for the government to support it.

Third, many eyes are watching the progress of the abovemen-tioned government policies. We are all aware of the great difference between announced policies and their actual implementation. The difference between policy announcement and its implementation has been observed many times in China in recent years. We are awaiting the implementation of the abovementioned market-oriented policies. I believe that the present Chinese government must have considered the implementation of these new policies before their announcement. There are many ways to help implement the above policies. Many of these polices will succeed if competition by private firms is allowed. To carry out such policies, the central government should be deter-mined to prevent the vested interests in different levels of the government from protecting the public enterprises and hindering the entrance of private firms. This is different from the implementation of government policies that requires the use of resources such as build-ing infrastructures which is not easier. The vested interests in protecting public enterprises from competition may be strong. Determination on the part of the central government is required to overcome them. We can only hope that the central government will have such determination in the implementation of its policy in expanding the role of private businesses in the Chinese economy.

CHAPTER 27

Important Considerations in the Urbanization of China

According to an article in the *New York Times*, June 16, 2013, China is moving 250 million people into newly constructed small cities and towns in the next 10 to 15 years. It will replace small homes with high risers. Growth is expected because income and consumption of city dwellers are higher than those of residents in the rural areas. People are given new apartments and money. It is the responsibility of the local governments to carry out this policy in their localities. In this chapter, I will discuss the important considerations useful for the implementation of this policy.

Let me first describe how urbanization has been achieved in the past. One important reason for the establishment of a city is its location, such as being close to a river or ocean that makes it convenient for the residents to travel and to trade. Examples are Shanghai, Nanjing and Guangzhou. Given its geographic advantage, the government often plays an important role in the building of its infrastructure, including roads, ports, and police protection. Urbanization occurs when there are economic gains from the concentration of economic activities in one location especially when the location is favorable as pointed above. Cities provide efficiency in the production of services, and to some extent production of physical commodities. When such economic activities take place in a city, the result is higher income for its residents. Rural people choose to move to cities mainly because they can earn a higher income there, leading to an increase in national income and consumption of the entire economy.

To illustrate, a person who decides to move to a city for his self-interest would calculate the economic gain from the move. Assume that if he decides to move, his income will change from 1,000 yuan to 1,800 yuan. The economic gain will be 800 yuan. Since his income is a part of the GDP of the economy, the latter will also increase by 800 yuan. Thus, urbanization will lead to an increase in income by 800 yuan. Since consumption depends on income, total consumption in the economy will also increase. This is the alleged reason for the Chinese government to introduce its policy of urbanization.

If by his calculation a person's income will decrease by 500 yuan after moving to an urban area, he will not move voluntarily. If the government forces him to move, his income will be reduced by 500 yuan. So will national income.

It may be suggested that the government can introduce policies to increase his urban income, such as providing housing, etc. In this case if he decides to move, it must mean that the compensation has to be at least 500 yuan. There will be a loss in national income by 500 yuan because the government has used up 500 yuan of national income and the move produces no change in the income of the person being forced to move.

In the case of China, farmers are unwilling to move to a city because of the lack of opportunities to work there to make a better living or because they will earn less by moving as described above. They prefer to stay in the rural area because they can use their land to make a living and retire there. They can make a living in their farms, while they need social welfare in cities to provide them with the same standard of living. Forcing the farmers to move to urban areas would reduce his income and national income. It will also create discontent and adversely affect the achievement of a harmonious society in China.

In conclusion, it is costly for the government to force citizens to move from the rural areas to the cities because in doing so, there will be a decrease in national income rather than an increase in economic growth. Forcing the farmers to move to cities will create discontent and affect the achievement of a harmonious society. In addition, government spending in this case may lead to inflation and an increase in bad debts of the government.

I hope that the above considerations will be helpful to the Chinese policy makers in the design to urbanize China and in the implementation of China's urbanization policy.

CHAPTER 28

Regulation of the Rate of Interest and Shadow Banking in China

It is well-known that the interest rate which commercial banks can pay to depositors is controlled by the government. As of February 2013, the interest rate paid by commercial banks to depositors was only 3% per year. The inflation rate as measured by the consumer price index increased by 4.6%, providing depositors with a negative real return for their deposits. A consequence of this policy is that some depositors would like to receive an interest rate higher than the regulated rate and at the same time, some borrowers or banks which can lend out the deposits are willing to pay a higher rate. The banks are willing to pay a higher rate because they can lend the money at an even higher rate to make a profit. Thus, the policy has created a shadow banking system paying a higher rate of interest than the official rate.

An article in the *New York Times* dated July 7, 2013, describes the phenomenon of this market where loans are made at a high interest rate. Text message solicitations began arriving on the mobile phones of many of China's wealthy last month, promising access to lucrative wealth management products with yields far above the government's benchmark savings rate.

One message read: "China Merchants Bank will issue a high interest financing product starting from June 28th to 30th. The duration of the product will be 90 days with a 5.5% interest rate. Please call us now." A day later came another. "The interest rate of yesterday's product has been raised to 6%. (Product duration is 90 days). There is limited access to this product. First come, first served."

The offers are not coming from fly-by-night operators but from some of China's biggest banks. They are raising huge pools of cash to finance a relatively new and highly profitable sideline business: lending outside the scrutiny of bank regulators.

China's regulators — and a fair number of economists, policy makers and investors — worry that legitimate banks are using lightly regulated wealth management products to repackage old loans and prop up risky companies and projects that might not otherwise be able to borrow money. Analysts warn that shadow banking is helping drive the rapid growth of credit in a weakening economy, which could lead to — in the worst situation — a series of bank failures.

Let us apply the tools of supply and demand in economics to understand this phenomenon. The supply of deposits depends on the rate of interest. The higher the rate of interest, the more money people will deposit in the banks. The demand for deposits also depends on the rate of interest. The lower the rate of interest, the more the banks will accept deposits. The equilibrium interest rate is the rate which makes the quantity supplied equal to the quantity demanded. In a free market without government regulation, the interest rate will reach this equilibrium rate. If the rate of interest is arbitrarily set below the equilibrium rate, the amount that the depositors are willing to supply is less than the amount that the banks wish to obtain. The difference (the quantity demanded minus the quantity supplied) is the shortage of deposits in the market. The shortage is the amount of deposits that the banks wish to obtain minus the amount that the depositors are willing to supply.

When there is a shortage in the supply of deposits, some banks are willing to pay a higher interest rate to attract more deposits for them to lend to borrowers who are willing to pay an even higher rate. This institution, known as the shadow banking system, helps to eliminate the shortage of loans supplied in the market for loans. It is beneficial to the economy because the new depositors are able to obtain a higher rate for their deposits and the new lenders can profit by charging an even higher rate to borrowers who need the loans to pay for any projects they wish to undertake. If shadow banking did not exist, potential lenders would have no opportunity to earn a higher interest by lending their money. At the same time, potential borrowers would have no opportunity to borrow money that they need. In conclusion, it is the government control of the interest rate below the market rate that causes the shortage of money available for projects that require the loans. The shadow banking system solves the shortage problem and benefits a group of depositors and a group of bankers. In a market economy, demand and supply determine the price in equilibrium which leads to an efficient allocation of resources, bank loans in this case. Any interference of the price system inevitably decreases economic efficiency by reducing the quantity supplied, in this case the amount of deposits to be used for investment or for other purposes.

I would like to discuss four possible criticisms against the shadow banking system.

1. In China, people are competing for loans possibly by illegal means such as bribing the loan officers. If the interest rate is market-determined, there is no need to bribe to get loans. If a loan officer asks a potential borrower to pay him bribes, the borrower can go to another bank because there is competition among the potential lenders to reach a market equilibrium.

    Now assume that there is an interest rate ceiling and the "black market" rate of interest in shadow banking is higher than the equilibrium rate. Borrowers in the market of shadow banking will not need to bribe because the interest rate in the black market is also in equilibrium with competition among the lenders. However, if you want to borrow from the legal market at the lower than equilibrium interest rate, you will need to bribe because more people want such low-interest loans. In conclusion, when there is an interest rate ceiling, borrowers need to bribe to get loans from the legal market but do not need to bribe in the shadow banking system. When there is no interest rate ceiling, there will be less need to bribe.

2. Inefficiency is said to occur when bribes are paid in the allocation of funds. As I have explained above, when there is an interest rate ceiling,

allowing the borrower to borrow money in the shadow banking system at a higher interest rate requires no bribes. At the same time, such borrowing is beneficial to him and the economy because loans as a resource will be used to achieve an economic objective. Free exchanges between lenders and borrowers, as exchanges taking place in shadow banking, are always efficiency-enhancing.

3.   Another issue is that there are financial risks associated with trading in the shadow banking system. Although the system allows for the efficient allocation of loanable funds, lending in the shadow banking system is riskier than in the regular banking system.

4.   There are many people objecting to a "black market" and shadow banking is considered a black market because it is against the law. In this case, it is the law that is inappropriate, or the regulation of the interest rate that is inappropriate. This regulation creates the black market or shadow banking.

In conclusion, I would like to ask, "What is the rationale for controlling the rate of interest, especially after a recent policy announcement of the Chinese government to let prices be market-determined?"

Recently, the Chinese government announced a policy to expand the role of private enterprises and to allow the market to determine prices. Allowing the market to determine the rate of interest should be a part of this policy. If the interest rate is market-determined and not regulated, the shadow loan market will disappear. Under this circumstance, any criticism of this market will no longer exist, including the criticisms discussed above.

After this chapter was written, the People's Bank of China has announced that in the near future, say within two years from March 2014, it will abolish the regulation of the rate of interest and allow it to be market-determined.

CHAPTER 29

Solving the Debt Problem of the Chinese Local Governments

Today, the local governments in China are said to have incurred a large amount of debt. How large is the total amount? How did the debts come about? Why are these debts a serious problem? If it is a serious problem, how can we solve it?

China's national income is 48 trillion renminbi. Its local government debt is estimated to be about 14 trillion or 30% of national income. The central government debt is 14.4% of national income. Therefore, total government debt is about 44% of national income. These percentages are not high as compared with the debt of the US government which is about 100% of national income. The problem of national debt of the United States is considered somewhat serious but not too serious by most of the people. The democrats do not consider it very serious while most republicans consider it more serious. Although China's local government debt is a small percentage of national income as compared with the US debt, its problem is considered serious because the local governments' ability to repay their debts is unreliable and the economic resources financed by the debt are not put into good use. Also, the American government debt is held by its people and by foreign countries that have faith that the US government will honor its debt. On the other hand, the Chinese local government debt is borrowed from the banks through publicly-owned enterprises which most often do not repay the debt. The Chinese central government is considered more trustworthy and its national debt is considered small because the central government has sufficient revenue from taxation to repay its debt.

How is the debt financed? Local governments borrow money by setting up special financing entities which will borrow money on their behalf. They use publicly-owned enterprises to borrow from state-owned banks. They obtain their funds by leasing (not selling because all land in China is publicly owned and cannot be sold) land to developers. The local governments help finance favored industries like the solar industry by allowing them to borrow even though such ventures are risky. They can accumulate such large amounts of debts because they can borrow from banks without paying them back.

What is wrong with having these debts? First, if their repayment is unreliable, they undermine the authority of the local governments and make it difficult for them to borrow money in the future when needed. Second, they also undermine the authority of the central government if the local governments are under the control of the central government. Third, if the loans are spent unwisely, economic resources are wasted. On the other hand, if the loans are wisely spent, they can help local economic development by building infrastructure such as high speed railroads which are financed by debt. Fourth, if the debts are borrowed from the banks, they lead to bad debts of the banks and make the banking system unstable.

How can we solve the problem? Some people suggest that the central government exercise a tighter control over the local governments. In fact, the central government has tried to do so. Recently, the national audit office under the State Council decided to conduct an audit of the debt incurred by local governments. It is questionable whether the control from the central government will be effective.

Since all loans are borrowed from the banks, a more effective solution is to improve the functioning of the banking system. Since economic reform started in 1978, the Chinese banking system has not been successfully reformed. It still maintains the practice of the period of central economic planning by extending loans to state-owned enterprises based on political and administrative considerations and not on economic considerations. Bad loans are not a serious problem for the banks because the government implicitly guarantees the solvency of the banks. The central government has set up asset management corporations to buy up some of the bad loans of the banks. The banks are allowed to extend loans fairly freely and unwisely. To solve the bad loans problem and the associated problem of bad debts of the local governments, it is necessary to limit the lending ability of the banks and to insure that the loans extended will be repaid. This is the case for a healthy banking system like the systems in the US and Hong Kong.

The banks in China should be financially independent entities regulated by the central bank. Financial independence should force the banks and their managers as well as employees to consider seriously their financial benefits. Extending an excessive amount of loans would expose the banks to financial risks. Extending loans for unworthy projects would reduce the profits of the banks and thus the compensation of their employees. In economic terms, the banks should be subject to a hard budget constraint. The economic incentives for the managers and employees are extremely important. Without economic incentives, they would extend loans based on personal and political considerations. One way to prevent this from happening is to have a bank issue stocks with majority shares owned by the public. The shareholders elect a Board to control the management of the bank. In a well-functioning banking system, the central bank or another monetary authority can regulate the amount of reserves held by the commercial banks and limit the amount of loans that they can extend. The economic incentives of the employees are well-established. Such a banking system not only helps the banks to achieve efficient allocation of financial resources but also enable the central government to conduct monetary policy in order to regulate the macroeconomy and reduce economic fluctuations. It will also reduce the bad debt of the state-owned enterprises and of the local governments so that they will use economic resources more efficiently.

CHAPTER 30

The Present and Future of the American Recession and Lessons for China

Since 2008, the US economic downturn has affected many other countries including China. The US recession is the subject of concern to many people and the topic of this chapter. In this chapter, I would like to discuss this topic as presented by a well-known American author Meredith Whitney in her book, *Fate of the States* (New York: Portfolio Hardcover, 2013). She became well-known in October 2007 when she predicted the coming of the US recession. I will (1) discuss the great recession as it is generally understood, (2) explain the viewpoint of Whitney's book and (3) point out the book's relevance to China's economic development policy.

Let me first discuss the general understanding of the US economic downturn. The behavior of consumers has an important effect on the US macroeconomy because it affects business investment. Both aggregate consumption and investment expenditures are parts of national income. Financial markets channel the savings of consumers to investment. Financial markets can collapse as a result of risk-taking behavior of consumers and investors.

In 2008, the real estate bubble in the United States burst. Property prices first increased and then dropped rapidly. The prices increased because consumers speculated on the increase in price by purchasing houses using mortgage loans without paying a down payment but at high interest rates. In order to supply the expanding volume of loans, banks and financial institutions packaged the mortgages into securities for sale to investors. This increased the funds for consumers, investors and financial institutions to speculate on real estate. When the bubble burst, consumers lost money and could not pay the interest on their mortgages. The values of mortgage loans and the associated securities declined so much so that financial institutions and investors holding such loans and securities incurred substantial losses. When the financial market collapsed, some of the largest financial institutions and banks had to close down. This affected the operation of the entire US economy. Observing the situation, the Federal Reserve and the Treasury Department decided not to allow the failure of some very large financial institutions and spent a large amount of taxpayers' money to save them but the American economy continued to experience a great recession. Those supporting the government policy to bail out the large financial institutions and the automobile manufacturers claimed that without such a policy the recession would have gone deeper. Those critical of the policy said that it cost the taxpayers a large sum of money without improving the economic condition substantially and at the same time, it encouraged similar irresponsible behavior of the financial institutions in the future.

With the above background, we can discuss the viewpoint of Meredith Whitney. As the title of her book suggests, her analysis focuses on the fate of states in the US, especially on their economic conditions during the great recession. Generally speaking, the real estate bubble and the economic downturn caused by the risk-taking behavior of local consumers, investors and financial markets affected the economic conditions of the state in which they resided. The downturn was most serious in the wealthiest states, such as California, Florida, Arizona, Nevada, Illinois and New Jersey. Their consumers, investors and the financial markets had the ability to engage in risky investments. Conversely, in the poorer states such as Iowa and Texas, the residents could not afford to engage in risky investments and the impact of the recession was smaller.

Meanwhile, the state governments themselves also behaved the same as their residents. Governments of the rich states invested heavily in real estate. After the bubble burst, the governments of these states were heavily in debt. They increased taxes and reduced government spending. After the taxes were raised, the state residents had less income and more debt. When the state governments reduced spending to provide services such as education and infrastructure building, employment in these states declined. Income and consumption expenditures in these states were reduced. This led to a vicious cycle. The reduction of income, employment and provision of government services caused some industrial enterprises to leave these states. The fate of the poorer states was much better.

In order to solve the problems of the US recession and to promote the development of the US economy, Whitney recommends the development of industries in the poorer states which are in better economic conditions. This would attract investment including foreign investment. The recommendation also includes the provision of training to increase human capital. The industrial development of these states is more important than the development of the financial sector.

What lessons can we learn from the above discussion for the development of the Chinese economy? The recession in China was much less serious. The annual growth rate of China's GDP was reduced only to about 7.6% or so from about 9.5% before the world recession. The reason was that China's consumers, financial markets and investors were not as risk-taking as those in the United States. Consumers were not accustomed to and not allowed to take a mortgage to purchase houses without a down payment. Mortgage loans were not packaged into securities to be sold to investors in financial markets. The growth of national income in China slowed down mainly because of reduction of exports due to the great recession in the US and other countries.

For China's economy to maintain a steady growth rate, we should consider two policy options. The first is to stabilize the economic activities of consumers, financial markets and investors and to prevent them from engaging in excessive risk-taking activities. The second is the further development of the industrial sector in China.

Regarding the first, we need not be concerned with the behavior of consumers. Chinese consumers do not take too much risk in speculating in the real estate market, and they are not allowed to purchase houses without paying a down payment. We should be concerned with the behavior of the investors, the financial institutions and local governments. Investors could take excessive risk in speculating in real estate to increase its price. So could the financial institutions. Because the Chinese government regulates the interest rate by imposing a ceiling, a shadow banking system has appeared to raise funds at a higher interest rate as discussed in Chapter 28. Loans in the shadow banking system tend to be riskier for both the borrowers and the lenders. Therefore, we should pay attention to the future development of China's financial institutions. The government should establish appropriate policies to regulate financial institutions and prevent them from taking on excessively risky investments. The Chinese banks should be made financially independent to prevent them from extending bad loans to state-owned enterprises and to local governments. The large amount of local government debt has presented a serious problem as discussed in Chapter 29.

On the development of industry, the size of the industrial sector tends to decline relative to the financial sector in the course of economic development. According to the *China Statistical Yearbook* (Beijing: National Bureau Statistics, 2012), in 1978 the sectors of agriculture, industry and services accounted for 28.2%, 47.9% and 23.9% of national income respectively. By 2000, these percentages became 15.1%, 45.9% and 39.0%. In 2012, they were changed to 10.1%, 45.3% and 44.6%.

Whether the service sector should be allowed to increase at the expense of the industrial sector depends on the components of the service sector. Teaching and research, technological innovation, transportation, communication and health care should be allowed to develop. The development of financial markets offering new risky financial instruments should be discouraged. It may be a prudent policy for China to extend the period of industrial development and to limit the risk-taking behavior of new financial institutions in order to prevent large fluctuations of the Chinese macroeconomy. Finally, China's state-owned enterprises should not be allowed to enjoy special advantages in obtaining loans from banks at the expense of private enterprises. This policy is consistent with the policy announced by Chinese Premier Li Keqiang to promote the development of private enterprises.

CHAPTER 31

Solving the Problems of Health Care and Education in the United States

The problems with the health care insurance, and primary and high school education system in the US are known to be very serious. On health care, the controversies arising from Obamacare are so serious as to cause a shutdown of the Federal government in October 2013 and a government debt crisis arising from Congress failing to raise the debt limit in late 2013. The primary and high school systems are so poor as to cause, at least partially, the low test scores and relative ratings of American children as compared with children in many other countries, including those with per capita income much lower than the US.

The main problem with health care is that many Americans do not have health insurance like many countries with lower per capita income, such as Canada, Taiwan and most European countries. In order to introduce universal health care, President Obama succeeded in proposing and having the US Congress pass a universal healthcare system known as Obamacare. The law requires all people to have health insurance. The health insurance must cover 10 core benefits. Many single persons and working families may receive assistance from the government to help pay for their insurance. Many state medical assistance programs, also known as Medicaid, should expand to offer health plans to more uninsured people. A new way to buy health insurance will be created, known as the Health Insurance Marketplace.

Insurance rates will depend on people's age, where they live, whether they smoke, and the health plan selected.

When the law came into effect in October 2013, several hundred thousands of people wishing to obtain Obamacare through the Internet could not register because the Internet designed by the government could not handle so many people. Some say that this shows the popularity of the program. Others say that this shows the inability of the government to run important programs. I believe that, even if most people are able to sign up for it, the program is defective in that it is forcing people to choose from a limited set of health insurance alternatives specified by the government and in introducing expensive and ineffective institutions to provide health care that people may not want. A better and much simpler solution is for the government to provide a voucher to every family which can be used to buy insurance from the market place as the family deems appropriate. Of course, the value of the voucher is limited just like the provision under Obamacare. It can be similar to the value provided by Obamacare. Under the voucher system, there is no need for the government to introduce health care institutions that provide health care which is likely to be expensive and inefficient without government subsidy. Under the voucher system, the free choice of the people in selecting the insurer will provide competition to make the providers efficient in charging lower cost and providing better benefits.

Under the current primary and high school education system, parents are required to pay property tax based on the value of their residence to support a public school system. Such a system provides poor education to the students because the school administrators and teachers have a monopoly in providing education. They perform poorly because their income is guaranteed by the tax revenue. I believe that the public school system with many low-quality administrators and teachers is the main cause for the poor performance of young American students as revealed in their low test scores as compared with students in many other countries. According to an article in the *New York Times* dated October 23 2013, a report released by the National Center for Education Statistics, an office of the Education Department, showed that even in the country's top-performing states — which include

Massachusetts, Vermont and Minnesota — the percentage of students that scored at the highest levels is smaller than the percentage in several East Asian countries. Except for the low-quality education, how can one explain the low test scores of American children when American parents are more educated on average than the parents living in countries with higher test scores? A partial explanation is that as a result of discrimination in the past, many African American children are raised in single-parent households and are not well motivated. But this problem applies only to a small fraction of the American population and cannot explain why the scores of the top American students are still below those in other countries as the above *New York Times* article reports.

Again, the solution to this education problem is for the local government which taxes its residents to use the tax revenue to provide a voucher to each family. This voucher can be used to pay for the cost of education provided by any school, public or private. Such a system would eliminate public schools with low quality because parents will not send their children to these schools. New private schools providing higher quality education will appear and parents will choose them. Again, competition among schools will insure high-quality education. A voucher will be provided to every family but the value of the voucher may depend on the amount of tax that the county of residence collects which depends on the income level of its residents. This is also true under the present system of public schools where the income of the schools is dependent on the income level of its residents.

At present, residents of a township tend to have similar income levels because families choose their residence according to the prices of housing that they can afford. A county with expensive housing tends to attract rich people and thus can collect higher property taxes to pay for education, whether under the voucher system or under the current system of public education. Any method to redistribute income among counties for the purpose of equalizing their education expenditures can be applied under the voucher system as under the present system of public schools. For example, the state government may use its tax revenue to subsidize the poor counties for the purpose of providing education as the Federal government has a progressive income tax system partly to redistribute income among US citizens.

The use of vouchers for consumers to pay for their basic necessities is an idea first suggested by my late teacher, the former Professor Milton Friedman of the University of Chicago. His idea is an effective and economically efficient way to pay for the necessities as it insures free choice and encourages competition among providers. The idea can be used to provide health care insurance and primary and high school education for US citizens and to provide other necessities as the situation requires. When there are problems similar to the health care insurance and education problems discussed in this chapter, we should consider this solution before designing other possibly less effective and less efficient methods. This idea is based on the basic principles in economics to encourage competition in production and to allow consumers a free choice to select their products.

CHAPTER **32**

Two Suggestions to Reform the Chinese Banking System

Today, China's banking system in general is functioning properly but there are two aspects that can be improved. The first is to increase the banks' reserve requirement to 100% of the loan. The second is to issue 1,000 yuan banknotes. Let us discuss these two proposals.

In 2008, the US recession began because of the collapse of its financial markets. The collapse was due to the risk-taking behavior of consumers, financial markets and investors. Consumers were willing to take risks in buying real estate without paying a down payment to the bank. Financial institutions packaged the bank loans as securities to sell to investors, and investors were willing to buy such risky securities. As a consequence, housing prices increased greatly. A housing bubble occurred when the prices of housing fell rapidly.

Many consumers and investors went bankrupt. The financial markets collapsed. National income was reduced in an economic downturn and unemployment increased. Some people believe that if we had reduced the risk-taking behavior mentioned above, the economic downturn would not have happened. A policy to reduce risk-taking behaviors and stabilize financial markets is to control the lending activities of the banks and other financial institutions. This can be done by introducing legislation and establishing government institutions to regulate financial markets. Another and more efficient way to solve the problem of risk-taking behavior is to change the operation of the banks by preventing them from over extending bank loans. This

143

can be done by increasing the bank's reserve requirement to 100% of its loans. Given such a reserve requirement, even if the consumers, financial markets and investors are willing to take risks, they will not be able to obtain the funds to do so. This policy will help stabilize the financial markets and prevent an economic downturn from occurring. The new policy will not affect the government's ability to increase the money supply in order to promote economic development, because the government would still control the supply of money.

In the early 1950s, when I was a graduate student at the University of Chicago, my teachers told me that to require its commercial banks to have 100% reserve for their loans is a very good way to stabilize financial markets and macroeconomic activities. The reason why the United States did not adopt this system was that its existing system of fractional reserve had become a tradition that was difficult to change. In the 1980s, when I served as adviser to the Chinese State Commission for Restructuring the Economic System, I gave serious consideration to the problem of bank reserve requirement. I consulted with a very distinguished colleague at the Department of Economics at Princeton University. He is now a top official in the US Federal Reserve. He also agreed that requiring the banks to have a 100% reserve was a desirable policy. I did not recommend this policy to the Commission for Restructuring of the Economic System because there were more important issues. Today I put forward this proposal because the United States has been experiencing a serious financial crisis and economic downturn due to the over extension of bank loans. Although the Chinese consumers, financial markets and investors are not as risk-taking as those in America, in the future the situation may change after further development of China's financial markets. Requiring bank loans to be backed by 100% reserve is a wise policy today. If the requirement of 100% reserves is considered too strict, it can be reduced to 80%.

A related policy is to determine the annual increase in money supply under any reserve requirement. Because national income continues to increase, it is necessary to increase money supply for the activities of production and consumption. However, the increase in money supply cannot be too rapid in order to avoid inflation.

To avoid inflation, how fast should money supply be increased? Should it be increased each year at the same rate as national income? The appropriate rate is determined by the income elasticity of demand for money. If the elasticity is equal to 1.2, when the national income is increased by 10%, the demand for money will increase by 12%. Increasing money supply by 12% will keep the price level constant and not cause inflation. According to the *China Statistical Yearbook* (Beijing: National Bureau of Statistics, 2012), from 1978 to 2012, the index of China's national income in real terms increased from 100 to 2422, or by 24.22 times, while currency in circulation increased from 212 to 54,600, or by 257.54 times. Since the price index increased by 10.648 times, the increase in money supply in real terms was only 257.54/10.648 = 24.187 times. Hence, the ratio of the percentage increase in money supply to the percentage increase in national income was 24.187/24.22 or approximately 1.00. This is the income elasticity of demand for money in China. Because the elasticity is equal to 1.00, if real national income increases by 10%, money supply can be increased by 10%, and the price level will remain unchanged. If the money supply increased by 14%, the price will increase by 14%/10%.

The second suggestion is very easy to implement. It will provide the Chinese people much convenience. Everyone knows that carrying many banknotes of 100 yuan RMB for business transactions is very convenient. If we issue one-thousand dollar banknotes, business transactions will become much more convenient. I remember that in around 1970, the Taiwan government issued only $100 bills, and bills of lower denominations. The reason was that government officials were afraid that issuing currency of higher denomination would cause inflation as they recalled the experience of serious inflation in 1948 when currencies of high denominations were issued. Several of us, members of Academia Sinica, recognized that inflation is caused by increasing the quantity of money supply too rapidly and not by issuing large denomination banknotes. As long as the quantity of money is controlled properly, regardless of the denominations of banknotes, inflation will not occur. Later we persuaded the government authorities in Taiwan to issue one-thousand dollar banknotes, giving the residents much convenience in business transactions. In the issuance of large denomination banknotes, people can go to the bank to exchange ten 100 yuan bills for one 1,000 yuan bill, so that the quantity of money remains unchanged and inflation will not occur. If 500 yuan banknotes are considered sufficient to provide convenience, 1,000 yuan banknotes might not be required.

In this chapter, the two suggestions for reforming the Chinese banking system are easy to implement. The first proposal to require 100% reserves will stabilize financial markets and reduce future economic fluctuations. Other countries have not adopted it because it is difficult to change the traditional institutions. China is adopting further economic reform. It is a good time for China to adopt this policy proposal to stabilize its financial markets in the future. The second proposal would be welcomed by the people as it provides convenience in their daily life.

PART 4

Social Problems

Comparing Chinese and American Universities

For many years, I taught at American universities, and from 1980 onward, I began to visit Chinese universities frequently. The comparison of Chinese and American universities is a topic of interest to me and many readers. Many Chinese are interested in going to or in sending their children to American universities to study.

America's top universities are the best in the world. The main reason is that during World War II many leading scientists and renowned scholars fled to the United States from Europe. The improving intellectual environment in the course of America's postwar prosperity provided opportunities for these scholars to flourish. The quality of a university depends mainly on the quality of its teachers.

In the US universities, creative scholars encourage their students to think independently. The relationship between teachers and students are more equal than in China. Professors and graduate students study together and learn from one another. In China, professors say they "direct doctoral students" while in the US, professors try to help students to think originally and creatively. In academic discussions, we observe mutual respect among scholars, professors and students alike. Some Chinese scholars like to claim that they are the best in the field.

About half of the students in the graduate schools in the United States are from foreign countries. The number of Chinese students in these schools is increasing continuously. The quality of the students in Chinese universities continues to improve. Hence, some Chinese students in American graduate schools are really very good.

In the early 1990s, the Hong Kong University of Science and Technology was the first to emphasize research and publication of research papers in Hong Kong. This had affected the academic standards of all other universities in Hong Kong. In recent years, many universities in China have followed the universities in the US in stressing the importance of research and requiring the publication of research papers. This policy has resulted in putting pressure on Chinese professors and has increased academic plagiarism among many of them, but the positive impact of the policy change is still greater than the negative impact.

Economics education in Chinese universities has been improving rapidly. In January each year, the American Economic Association has its annual meeting. Doctoral students in the job market go to the meeting to look for jobs. In the past few years, about 35 Chinese universities sent people to this meeting to recruit young faculty members. China's top universities can pay PhD graduates in economics the world market salaries and are very competitive in the recruitment process. Some more experienced foreign scholars are also recruited by the top Chinese universities. China's best schools of economics are comparable in quality to some American departments of economics. For subjects other than economics, the quality of Chinese universities is not as good as for economics. Professors of these subjects tend to keep their own PhD graduates to continue working in the university and are less inclined towards hiring teachers from outside. The salaries are lower than for the economics professors. In the meantime, many Chinese students prefer not to return home to teach after obtaining their PhD in the United States.

To understand the rapid development of economics education, we can use the economic theory of supply and demand. On the supply side, in the 1980s, I cooperated with China's Commission of Education to organize graduate courses in economics held at Renmin University and Fudan University, which were known as the Ford classes. I also cooperated with the Commission to recruit and place graduate students in China to pursue PhD degrees in American and

Canadian universities. These two programs helped train a large number of qualified economists. On the demand side, as China experiences rapid economic development, it has created the need for graduates in economics to work in universities, the private sector and different levels of the Chinese government.

The Chinese Ministry of Education, in spite of economic reform in other sectors of the economy, continued to exercise strict control over the Chinese universities. It has limited the independent decision making of the universities in the same way as was the practice during the period of central planning. For example, the student enrollment of a school of business administration and the size of its faculty members require the approval of the Ministry of Education. However, a capable dean of a school is able to bypass these regulations in order to enhance the quality of the school. In China, "men can accomplish any task" also applies to higher education. Able Chinese educators can get around administrative obstacles and promote innovations at universities. I have visited the Wang Yanan Institute for Studies in Economics at Xiamen. I found that the Institute's academic environment is excellent and is comparable to that of a good American university. Faculty members and graduate students at the Institute have done research with me and co-authored some papers.

In the long term, we can expect the quality of teaching and research in Chinese universities to improve steadily. China's rapid economic growth and increasing market demand for good universities, together with its cultural tradition of respect for scholarship and learning, will help improve the quality of university education. Perhaps after some years, the quality of China's best universities will match the quality of many American universities.

CHAPTER 34

Have the Chinese People Restored their Pride?

China has become the world's second largest economy. When countries in Europe and North America suffered from a serious recession, China's economic growth continued and attracted much attention from the rest of the world. Member countries of the European Union are trying to get loans from China to save their fragile economy. In the summer of 2013, the United States tried to reestablish its influence in the Western Pacific region, mainly to counteract China's initiatives in this area. These initiatives appear to be excessive in the eyes of the United States. Undoubtedly, the world believes that China is now a very important country.

Many Chinese people are proud of their achievements. Historically, since the Opium War in 1840, China suffered from the signing of many unequal treaties, was defeated in the 1895 Sino-Japanese War, allowed Japan to occupy Manchuria and suffered from Japan's full-scale invasion in 1937. After many such experiences, the Chinese people felt deeply oppressed and humiliated. The question is whether the Chinese people now feel confident enough to get rid of the feeling of inferiority accumulated in the past.

The answer varies. Recently, I attended a lecture at Princeton University. The speaker is a political scientist at Harvard University and a native-born American. He claims that since the Western powers in the late Qing Dynasty humiliated the Chinese people, the sense of humiliation still affects the Chinese government's current foreign policy. In Western countries, some people think that China still keeps this stigma. From my own observations of the words and deeds of Chinese friends, I think that the majority of Chinese people, especially the younger generation not having experienced the humiliation from the Western powers, are no longer troubled by the old-fashioned thinking of a troubled past. They now have much self-confidence. I am asking this question because the Chinese people I know may be a biased sample and I have not discussed this topic of self-confidence with them.

My personal experience may affect my judgment of the view of Chinese people and make my opinion biased. As an American having lived a comfortable life for many years, I may have gotten rid of any sense of humiliation brought about by China's recent history. I also realize that my personal views and the views of many Chinese people may not be the same. The first example is China's successful bid to host the 2008 Olympics when the whole nation was rejoicing. While people across the country celebrated this event, I did not think that it was a big deal. Smaller countries like Spain have also received such an honor. In this incident, China still needed to be recognized by the outside world as a host of the Olympic Games. The second example is the Shanghai World Expo that was held in 2010. For this World Expo, the Shanghai municipal government and the public had invested a lot of manpower and resources. Note that the US government did not pay much attention to the US Pavilion until at the last moment before the opening, Mrs. Hillary Clinton decided to raise fund for the project. The 2008 Olympics came and went. So did the 2010 Shanghai World Expo. Both activities were very successful! People around the world have recognized these activities. The Chinese people are very proud of them.

We may ask how many times such successes are required for the Chinese people to get rid of their feeling of humiliation from recent history and to develop a sense of self-confidence. The answer depends on one's own view. As a scholar, I could conduct a survey of the Chinese population to find the answer. Since I have not conducted such a survey, I would like to put this question forward to the readers to ponder. In addition, I would like to remind those who are still plagued by the years of humiliation in the past to think of China's recent achievements which may make us proud enough to erase the bad memories of the past. In the 17th century and before, the Chinese people were always confident and proud. Now, with the same degree of self-confidence and pride, the Chinese people not only can determine their own destiny but also help people in other parts of the world to improve their economic and social conditions.

CHAPTER **35**

News of the American Presidential Election

This chapter was written in October 2012.

The American presidential election will be held on Tuesday, November 6, 2012. It will be the 57th presidential election in which presidential electors elected by the voting citizens in their district will actually elect the President and the Vice President of the United States on December 17, 2012. It is now the most important subject in newspapers and television talk shows. In this chapter, I will discuss the nature, content and significance of the reports in the news media. I will also comment on the effects of the election outcome on the US economy and US-China relations.

At present, the race between President Obama and Mitt Romney appears to be close. The most important question is who will win. This question is answered by looking at the preferences or likely choice of different types of voters. The voters are classified by gender, age group, race, state of residence, profession, etc. For example, workers tend to prefer Obama as a Democrat whereas business executives tend to prefer Romney as a Republican. Young people are likely to vote for Obama. Latinos tend to vote for Obama. The preference of women is about evenly distributed. It is suggested that the preference of women is influenced by how much they like the wife of the candidate. Such information is obtained by a number of polls conducted periodically by major news media such as *NBC*, *New York Times*, *CBS* and the *Wall Street Journal*. A poll will ask each respondent questions to compare the two candidates: for example, who will provide better leadership in the conduct of economic affairs, whether the respondent thinks his economic condition has improved since Obama became President, and whether he has already made up his mind on his vote, and if so, whom will he vote for.

An important factor determining the outcome of the American presidential election has been studied extensively in the last three decades. It is the economic conditions of the country in the period within six months of the election. If the economic conditions are favorable, the voters are happy and will tend to vote for the current President. Quantitative economics and quantitative political science methods have enabled a quantitative study of this factor. At present, this factor does not clearly favor either candidate because the economic signals are mixed. On the positive side, the annual rate of GDP growth has improved to over 2.3% but the unemployment rate has remained as high as 8.3% with a slow rate of new jobs being generated in the market. Obama can also claim credit for saving the American Automobile industry which received substantial financial support by his administration three years ago. At the same time, the price of oil is high. Either candidate can select economic evidence to support his case. Therefore, we cannot predict the outcome of the election by economic factors this time.

What is the significance of the result of this election to the American citizens? A Republican president will tend to make the role of the Federal government in the economy smaller. He would try to dismantle some of the active government policies enacted during the Obama administration. Such policies include the health care bill that requires all Americans to buy health insurance. This requirement is also being reviewed by the Supreme Court as it was being challenged as being unconstitutional. The policies also include new regulations that impose restrictions on the activities in Wall Street. If Obama is re-elected, he would try to keep the above policies and perhaps even allow the government to play a more active role such as increasing the income tax rate of the very rich citizens. However, it is my judgment that such policies will have minor effects on the rate of growth of US

GDP although some may have an important effect on the distribution of income and bring about a sense of fairness in the American economy.

It is also my belief that the outcome of the election will not have any major effect on US-China relations. Both parties will have to consider China as a major power, deal with China as an equal, seek China's cooperation in major issues such as containing Iran and North Korea, and compete with China not only in the Western Pacific but all over the world where China has its sphere of influence which is now worldwide.

CHAPTER 36

American Democracy in the Light of the State of the Union Address

In the State of the Union speech delivered on February 12, 2013, the US President listed a number of important tasks for the US government to perform, including the construction of infrastructure, the development of education, improving health care, raising the minimum wage level and the legislation of immigration law. Among them, the legislation of immigration law is necessary not only to curb illegal immigration, but also to attract skilled migrants with specific skills.

The President's speech was broadcast and aired on all TV stations. Immediately afterwards, the content of his speech was questioned from a different point of view. This view was expressed by Rubio, a Republican congressman from Florida. Although Rubio did not specify what measures he opposes, and the reasons for the objection, he pointed out that the President's speech was filled with various measures taken by the government in the intervention of the American economy, but failed to state by how much these measures will increase the government deficit. In the *New York Times* on February 21, 2013, a headline news reported that the Republican majority in the House of Representatives was attempting to slash spending stated in domestic legislative proposals.

Respect for civil liberties and the rights of individuals and limiting the power of government are the cornerstone of American democracy. In practice, constraints on government power are achieved through the two-party system. Through the election of the President to lead

161

the executive branch of the government and the elections of members of the US Congress, US citizens exercise their rights in a democratic system of government. They can choose between members of two parties in both the executive branch and the legislative branch of the government. In the legislative branch, each state is represented by two senators in the Senate and by a number of congressmen in the House of Representatives. Each congressman represents his/her constituency and is elected by voters in his/her congressional district. Thus, the more populous the state or the larger the number of congressional districts, the larger the number of House Representatives can be elected.

Under this political system, important policies proposed by the President and members of his party must be approved by the House and the Senate to be implemented, including the items mentioned in President Obama's State of the Union address. Congressmen having different views often represent the positions of their respective political parties. This difference often leads to the failure in implementation of projects proposed by the President. Thus, from the perspective of implementation of the President's policies, the US democratic system is inefficient. Some of the President's proposed projects cannot be passed by Congress and do not get implemented. As a result, in the United States controversial matters of the two political parties cannot receive the support of the Congress to become legislation. On the other hand, the system of checks and balances in the American government effectively avoids serious abuse of power, a phenomenon that often appears in a strong centralized government.

In contrast, mainland China's political system is more efficient. The decisions that are made by only a few people who belong to the same political party will not be opposed by another party. But the lack of checks and balances also allows low-quality projects to be passed. For example, some have questioned the current government policy of possibly excessive intervention in the market economy. State-owned enterprises receive favorable treatments as compared with private enterprises. In the 1990s, China's state-owned enterprises and private enterprises seemed to compete in a more equal environment. However, since about 2000, state-owned enterprises have received government support, including access to loans from state-owned banks.

During my visit to Taiwan, on hearing Obama's speech on February 12, 2013, I began to think of writing about its democratic system. Under the non-democratic leadership of Chiang Kai-shek and Chiang Ching-kuo, Taiwan's government was efficient in the formulation and implementation of its policies for the economic development of the Taiwan economy. In 1986, Chiang Ching-kuo approved the formation of the Democratic Progressive Party, or the DPP. In 1988, on the death of President Chiang Ching-kuo, vice president Lee Teng-hui succeeded Chiang Ching-kuo to become president. In 1996, after the first general election in Taiwan, Lee Teng-hui was elected President. Today, in a democracy, members of Taiwan's legislative body, behaving like the US lawmakers, raise objections to the economic policies proposed by the executive branch of the government and do not allow them to be approved. In addition, when a president's term is up and cannot be re-elected, he will assert his influence to make his party win more votes in the coming election. This is done by pursuing projects that have short-run or immediate effects and objecting projects that may result in longer term benefits to the economy, such as an increase in the price of oil that is below market price, or a needed increase in taxes, etc. Useful and important projects for long-term economic development tend to be ignored.

In this chapter, I have presented some positive and negative aspects of the political systems in United States, China and Taiwan in terms of the efficiency in the formation and implementation of policies, especially policies for economic development. Readers may disagree with some of the views expressed above. I would be pleased if the ideas presented above could lead to further thinking on the part of the readers.

CHAPTER 37

Management and Cooperation

I am fortunate to have a good friend who has had much experience as a senior manager of major corporations, in the field of high-technology for computer related products, such as Apple and Hewlett Packard. He told me that his successful experience as a manager is based on three principles in directing people under him to work. These principles are (1) defining very clearly the objectives of the tasks to be performed to each member of the group, (2) motivating each person to perform the tasks, and (3) treating each person fairly in the way of rewarding and disciplining them. The discussions on these three principles should be open. It is easy for any person to understand these principles but very few people have the ability to carry them out. That is why only very few people are capable of becoming a senior manager in a large corporation. The abilities of a manager also include the ability to deal with people, understand the nature of the tasks that his group has to perform and understand the abilities and limitations of members of his group in performing the tasks. A senior manager has under him a number of lower level managers. Hence, the above remarks apply to his relationship with these lower level managers.

I have not been and am not qualified to be a senior manager of a large corporation but I have had some success in getting work done in cooperation with other people. For example, I was co-chairman of the US-China Committee on Economic Education and Research in China. The Committee received financial support from the Ford Foundation in the order of US$1 million each year from 1985 to 1995 and supported an Economic Training Center at Renmin

University from 1985 to 1996 and a second Center at Fudan University from 1987 to 1993. Each center trained about 50 graduate students in economics each year, who were selected by the Education Commission (now the Ministry of Education) and were taught by professors from the US. The committee worked well because the other members had high qualifications as economists and they also wanted to help develop modern economics in China.

I have gotten a lot of important work done during my lifetime by following one important principle: I seek out people to work with me only when I find these people to have the same interest in performing the tasks at hand as I do. I have never tried to persuade another person to do something I wish to get done unless it is also of benefit to him. If the other person has the same interest, there is no need for me to persuade him. The cooperation will be a success because both of us wish to get the work done. There is no need for me to have the talents of a manager as described in the first paragraph. As an implication of the above principle, I do not give favor to people who ask me to persuade someone whom I know well to help them, unless the help is also of interest to the people providing the help.

I can recommend to the readers that if you do not have the talents to be a manager as described in the first paragraph, you can still get a lot of work done if you choose only those people who have the same desire to complete the task at hand as you to work with you (the stronger their desire, the better). There are still plenty of important tasks that can be accomplished if you follow this principle. Of course, you yourself need to have some talents in the tasks to be performed. Otherwise, others will not wish to work with you because you will have little to contribute in such a cooperation.

38

Reflections on the Progress of Taiwan's Society

From the end of July to August 17, 2012, I visited the Institute of Economics of Academia Sinica and the Taiwan Semiconductor Manufacturing Company (TSMC). From my friends, I have learned that social life in Taiwan has improved a great deal in the last 20 years. People are more orderly when taking public transportations than before. The reason is partly economic. For example, the building of a convenient subway system in Taipei and the construction of fast trains enable more people to travel without having to compete for space. My friends told me that they were living more happily today than a decade or so ago. Most of them prefer Taipei to Beijing as a city for residence.

Orderly conduct in the use of public facilities improves when more facilities are available. I often tell a story about my visit to Zhongshan University in Guangzhou in 1982. I needed to send a telegram to inform my host at Wuhan University the time of my arrival. My host at Zhongshan University took me to a post office and offered to send the telegram for me. At first, I insisted on sending it myself but was unable to get in front of a crowd of people submitting their telegrams. I finally gave up and asked my friend to send it for me.

Another instance occurred only about two years ago at the Jinan train station. I was taking a train from Jinan to Beijing. While waiting at the train station, I saw crowds of people rushing to get ahead of others to board the train as soon as they heard the announcement that the gate was open. I could not understand why these people were in such a hurry since each had a ticket for an assigned seat. I asked the woman sitting next to me in the waiting room. She said this was the way people in China behaved.

In the 1980s, China had gone through a period of shortage of consumer goods. People were eager to get their share of consumer goods and did not behave in an orderly fashion. Their behavior improved along with rapid economic growth and the increase in supply of consumer goods. Then came the behavior associated with opportunities to get rich. Many people became very eager to make money. In the process of getting rich, they are willing to break some rules at the expense of others. This partly accounts for the rampant corruption and for the disorderly behavior in business activities in China.

Historically, it takes years for people in poor societies to learn civil behavior after they became rich. It also takes years for the new rich to be gentle and kind to others, especially to their competitors. As the economic conditions in China continue to improve, civil behavior will come eventually. If we want to speed up the process, both the government and the people will need to make special efforts to promote a civil society. The government can increase supply of public transportation facilities. For example, the availability of fast trains between Shanghai and Hangzhou will reduce the congestion in the trains for ordinary citizens and facilitate their orderly behavior. The Chinese Communist Party has also tried to promote social harmony as its top priority.

Leaders in the Chinese society can also contribute to social harmony and good behavior. The Commonwealth (天下) Magazine of August 10–23, 2011, includes interviews of several leading Taiwan entrepreneurs. The Chairman of TSMC discussed how TSMC can fulfill its social responsibilities. The responsibilities include moral values, commercial standards, environmental protection and social welfare. The company has set up a cultural foundation to promote Taiwan's cultural activities and encourage its employees to be socially responsible as well. Such examples should be useful for China's social development.

Economic development has made the Chinese people richer and affected their social life. Taiwan's economic development took place earlier. It enabled the people in Taiwan to improve their social and cultural life. By contrast, China's economic development has occurred later. The improvement of social and cultural life in China still lags behind the improvement in Taiwan.

CHAPTER 39

Observing Taiwan for 46 Years

I returned to Taiwan recently to participate in the 30th meeting of Academia Sinica. Since 1970, I have attended all such meetings which are scheduled once every two years. I first visited Taiwan in 1966, some 46 years ago when I gave lectures at the Institute of Economics of Academia Sinica on econometrics. Based on my experience in the last 46 years since 1966, it may be worthwhile for me to record some of my reflections.

I was invited to visit Taiwan in 1996 because the Taiwanese government welcomed overseas Chinese scholars to participate in the work of economic development and treated them as the people of Taiwan. In 1966, Taiwan was quite poor. In Academia Sinica, most of the current buildings did not exist then. My family and I were invited to stay in a Japanese-style house near the Academy. Water buffalos roamed around outside our residence. The Institute of Economics was one of the very few institutes having its own building. I stayed there to do my research.

Taiwan's economic development was successful partly because some of the most talented people in different fields had moved to Taiwan from the Chinese mainland at the end of China's civil war. These people in government service included George Yeh, Yen Chia-kan, Sun Yun-hsuan, Shen Chong-han, Yu Kuo-hwa and others in the government. Dr. Hu Shih was President of Academia Sinica but unfortunately he passed away from a heart attack during a meeting of the Academia. Wang Shijie served as President of the Academy later. Chien Shiliang served as the President of National Taiwan

University. I was fortunate to have the opportunity to work with some of these people in the development of Taiwan's economy and to learn from them.

My work with the Taiwanese government started when several overseas economists including Ta-chung Liu of Cornell University, S. C. Tsiang of the University of Rochester, Tony Koo of Michigan State University, John Fei of Yale University and myself were appointed economic advisors by the then President Chiang Kai-shek in 1967. We returned to Taiwan every summer to work with a group of five important economic officials of the Executive Yuan on policies for Taiwan's economic development. Every summer, our work began with a series of meetings with the five economic officials of the Taiwan government from Monday to Friday. The five government officials included the Secretary of the Executive Yuan, the Head of Central Bank, the Minister of Economic Affairs, the Minister of Finance and the Director General of Accounting and Budget. The meetings lasted from 9 to 12 in the morning to discuss the important economic problems. Later, the visiting economists did research for about two months to find solutions to the problems and met again with the five government officials to propose and discuss the solutions. After reaching an agreement, the visiting economists wrote up the proposed solutions which were published in newspapers. The policy recommendations received support from the people in Taiwan partly because they were the result of serious discussion and deliberation among government officials and the visiting economists who were highly respected in the Taiwan society.

Another aspect of Taiwan's economic development is the introduction of technology. Dr. K. T. Li's great contribution in this regard was the establishment of the Science Park in Hsinchu. It helped introduce electronic and related technologies. This policy is different from the policy for the government to establish state-owned enterprises to apply the technology. Rather, the policy was for the government to provide technology and help the establishment of private enterprises using the technology. Under this policy, the government also recruited outstanding entrepreneurs from the United States to return to Taiwan to establish the enterprises. One of the most successful examples was Dr. Li inviting Dr. Morris Chang from the US to return to Taiwan, first to head the Hsinchu Science Park and later in 1987 to establish the Taiwan Semiconductor Manufacturing Company with initial financial support from the government. The company is now the largest semiconductor foundry in the world.

Today, the contribution of overseas scholars to Taiwan's economic development is much more limited than in the past for two reasons. First, there are already many talented people in Taiwan. Second, the role of the government in Taiwan's economic development is more limited. There are also two reasons for this. First, Taiwan now has a democratic government, making it more difficult for the government to formulate and implement economic policies. Second, Taiwan's economy has become highly developed, making it difficult to achieve further development. Of course, the Taiwan government still welcomes overseas scholars to return to help Taiwan's economic development. At each meeting of the members of Academia Sinica, there are policy recommendations prepared and publicized in newspapers.

The government in mainland China also welcomes overseas scholars to return to China to offer their service. There are a number of policies to achieve this objective, including the two thousand talents policy. Under this policy, academic institutions can propose talented Chinese persons overseas to return to China to serve at fairly high salaries. In general, these returnees are younger than those returning to Taiwan to offer their service in the 1970s, because China was able to send students to study abroad only after 1980. However, many young returnees from China have already made contributions in government and educational institutions, including their ideas for China's economic development.

Finally, let me comment on the relation between the Chinese mainland and Taiwan. Economic integration consists of four elements, namely trade, investment, migration of people and technology which is brought about by the first three. The two economies have been integrated in all four areas. In the 1980s, Taiwanese investment in mainland China promoted the economic development of China. After 1990, the Chinese economy has greatly improved. Bilateral trade and investment are good for both economies. Personnel exchanges also increased. People from China residing in the US have been elected members of Academia Sinica. The mainland government welcomes people from Taiwan to participate in its economic development, including some former high-ranking officials in the Taiwan government. Taiwan's government has not been as open-minded in welcoming people from the mainland possibly for fear of the political influence that they may assert. There is no doubt that mutual exchanges between these two economies will continue to increase.

CHAPTER 40

Lining Up in China

China is recognized to be one of the world's fastest growing economies, but every Chinese knows that China has serious social problems. I will discuss one of the serious social problems and suggest a solution.

One serious problem is that many Chinese citizens do not follow order or rules. I experienced this problem for the first time when I visited the Sun Yat-sen University in Guangzhou in 1980. I needed to send a telegram to my host in Wuhan which was the next stop of my travel. My host was a professor of Sun Yat-sen University, also my former classmate in China. He suggested that he would send the telegram for me and I said I would prefer to do it myself. At the post office, people coming to send a telegram did not line up. Instead, they crowded in front of the service window. It was simply impossible for me to hand in my telegram through the window. Finally, I agreed to let my friend send it for me. He pushed forward to get in front of the crowd and succeeded in sending the telegram.

My second experience occurred in 2007 when I was waiting in the Jinan train station to board a train to Beijing. As soon as people heard the broadcast that the boarding was to begin, people rushed toward the gate although everyone had a reserved seat.

Another experience took place at the Shanghai airport. In November 2012, I was to take a Continental Airline flight from Shanghai back to Newark which has an airport close to Princeton University. As soon as people heard the announcement that passengers having seat numbers between 20 and 30 can begin boarding, passengers having other seat numbers started to push in front of the line. After entering the aircraft, people did not follow order. Some tried to store their luggage by using their elbows to push other passengers aside. This made it difficult for the US flight attendants to offer their service in a friendly manner. I had not seen such happening before during years of travel on Continental Airline.

The problem I mentioned is well-known in China. Cultural habits are hard to change. In the 1930s through the 1940s when I grew up in China, the social behavior was much better than now. In the early 1950s, such bad habits had not developed. These habits were developed in a period of material deprivation, followed by a period of economic development when people fanned for themselves. I understand that it is difficult to change social habits in a short time, but it is possible to do so by applying an effective strategy and putting more resources. I would like to propose the following steps for consideration:

Step 1: A new law should be established, making disorderly behavior in post offices, railway stations, airports, parks and other public places illegal and the offender will receive severe punishment. Everyone must queue up to receive services. Crowding ahead of other people to obtain service will be illegal and subject to punishment.

Step 2: Police or other law enforcement personnel should be stationed at important locations where such illegal behavior is likely to occur. At each location, there must be sufficient law enforcement officers to enforce the law. If the budget is not sufficient to enforce the law in all strategic locations, a smaller number of locations should be selected to insure that at each strategic location there are sufficient officers to enforce the law.

Step 3: If the law enforcement officers cannot perform their duties, any citizen can report to the designated departments and get rewarded. Reporting by the news media should also be encouraged and rewarded.

Step 4: Each level of the government should report annually to the level above, from local to city, from city to provincial and from provincial to the central government, the state of implementation of this law. The reports should be publicized in the news media. Improvement in implementation of this law should be rewarded.

The above steps might appear to be too severe for such a small offence as not lining up properly. In practice, the legislation to make such offense illegal may be sufficient. To what extent the other three steps need to be taken depends on whether enforcement of the law requiring orderly behavior can be achieved without taking them. These steps are suggested to provide specific means to insure that the law will be successfully enforced. In China, we are hoping to build a harmonious society. To establish orderly behavior among the people is one aspect in the building of a harmonious society.

CHAPTER 41

Let the People Participate in Eliminating Corruption

At least for a decade, corruption by government officials has been a widespread phenomenon. The central government has made serious attempts to control it by punishing the serious offenders but without much success. Recently, the government has forbidden the use of public funds to entertain in restaurants. Most recently, the government declared a policy to stop the construction of office buildings for five years. I hope this policy will be successful but we are uncertain. In the meantime, the government also wants to get the support of the Chinese people to expose corruption. The purpose of this chapter is to develop this idea further in order to insure the success of the government policy to eliminate corruption.

I would like to suggest that ordinary citizens, newspaper reporters and even fellow government officials be provided economic incentives to expose corrupt officials. They will receive half of the money which the corrupt official has taken illegally from the government. If the judicial system is inadequate in enforcing these rules under the law, some new supervisory departments under the central and local governments may be needed to enforce the law. In addition, when one government official comes forward to expose another official, his past offense will be forgiven for the most part. This rule is similar to the current practice of catching criminals by offering their partners incentives to expose them.

There are three possible reservations in putting the above proposal into practice.

First, if there is no guarantee that the one who exposes the official is safe, such mechanism will not work. One recent case happened at Guangdong. When an individual exposed local officials of their corruption on the Internet, he was physically tortured, lost his right eye and was severely injured. To prevent this from happening, the central government and the local governments, under the order of the central government, should establish a system, including the legal system and possibly another branch of the government, to protect the individuals who expose corruption. In addition, the economic incentives will encourage many people to help fight corruption even if some others are afraid of possible harm inflicted on them. At the beginning when such a policy is implemented, many people will not come forward because of fear of punishment. It is through examples from the working of the system that people will gradually come forth to help implement it.

Second, the proposal may bring out the evil part of human nature. In the Cultural Revolution, people were encouraged to expose each other. At that time, it created so many tragedies that sons exposed fathers, wives exposed husbands and so on. Hence, there is a danger that encouraging people to expose each other may turn the morale standard to a low level. I would like to point out that the current situation is different. The behavior during the Cultural Revolution was destructive and illegal while the behavior to expose corrupt officials in the above proposal is constructive and legal. At present, corruption is so rampant in China that we need (1) the assistance from the people and (2) strong incentives for them to do so.

Third, even if these methods work, as long as the social institutions are still the same, one corrupt official will be replaced by another official as illustrated by many such instances in Chinese history. In the present case, corruption of one official will not be followed by corruption of another official taking the former's position because of fear of similar punishment.

Some people may think that corruption is so deep-rooted today and it will take a long time to be eliminated. However, efforts in the direction of giving people incentives to expose corrupt government officials will speed up this process. In the meantime, people will develop honesty and respect for the law. Such behavior will follow the rules of punishment and reward if the rules are practiced repeatedly.

This chapter has presented only preliminary ideas to fight corruption. These ideas need to be modified carefully to form a concrete policy. The policy needs to be implemented step by step. Time and experience are required to reduce corruption in China.

CHAPTER

42

Three Important Qualities Required for an American President

During the 2008 election, I voted for Barack Obama enthusiastically. He is very intelligent. He was a top student of the Harvard Law School and served as editor of the *Harvard Law Review*. He is charming and likeable. As a great orator, he attracts attention when he speaks. He was able to convince a large number of young Americans to vote for him. In the 2012 presidential election, I also voted for him but less enthusiastically. Now his popularity is at an all-time low.

A November 25 2013 *Reuters* report states, "A growing number of Americans doubt President Barack Obama's ability to manage the nation, according to a CNN/ORC poll released on Monday that reflects the possibly larger impact of his administration's fumbled rollout of its health care law. The poll also found that 53% of those polled said Obama is not honest or trustworthy, marking the first time that the CNN/ORC polling found a clear majority questioning the President's integrity, CNN said. 40% of the 843 US adults surveyed in the telephone poll early last week said Obama can manage the government effectively, down 12 percentage points from June. The poll was conducted on November 18–20 amid ongoing problems plaguing the President's signature domestic policy achievement, the health care law widely known as Obamacare."

From Obama's record I discovered that under the American democratic system to elect presidents by major votes obtained in electoral districts, a person elected may not have the abilities required to serve as President. I then began to think that being a very intelligent person and a charming speaker who can gather votes are not sufficient conditions for a good President. I have concluded that three conditions are necessary for being an effective President.

The first is the quality of leadership and the ability to administer. It is the ability to direct people to work hard for the objective one has selected. Such leadership skill is required for the leader of any large organization such as a large cooperation or a university, and for a governor of a state in the US and a governor of a Chinese province. The leader needs to make clear what needs to be done and what the reward for success and the punishment for failure are.

The second is to have a vision and good judgment on the direction or policy to be pursued. Determining the objective for the organization to pursue is as important as administrative and leadership skill. In the case of US health care insurance, Obamacare is the result of poor judgment concerning what the American public desires. It is therefore not a desirable policy to pursue. The policy would be unpopular even if the insurance registration through the Internet did not encounter serious problems. Many US citizens simply do not like this program. Its failure has led to the closing of the US government for 16 days and the threat of default in paying the US government debt.

The third requirement is an understanding of how the American political system works. Knowing the right direction to pursue is not enough. An American President needs to know how to work through the American two-party system and to get the support of members of both parties in the US Congress to get a legislation approved and implemented. He needs to understand the process by which the required legislation can be obtained.

In the case of an MD, knowing the required operation is not enough. He needs to know how to perform the operation. A professor is good at understanding the nature of a subject but in most cases does not have the first two qualities. He may be good in teaching and research but may not be able to manage a university or to judge a desirable direction for the university to pursue.

The first two qualities apply to the leader of any large organization but in the case of an American President, the working of the American political system is important. Understanding the working of the two-party system is not required for a CEO of a large corporation or a president of a large university.

It is interesting to ask whether the required qualities of a good leader, as stated above, are innate or can be obtained by training. I believe they are innate. Considering the case of Obama, one may say that he did not have sufficient training and experience before becoming President. However, even after serving as President for five or six years, he still does not have these qualities. In general, if these qualities could be obtained by training, there would be more people capable of being a leader of a large corporation or a large university than there are available today. The qualities of being a good administrator and having sound judgment about the direction that the organization should work toward are different. Having the former alone would qualify a person to serve as a vice president of a large organization but not the president. Having the second qualification alone enables a person to serve as an adviser to the President but not the President.

Name and Subject Index

Printed in the United States
By Bookmasters